CW01083511

I'LL LOVE YOU FOREVER

Rita Beggins

Grosvenor House
Publishing Limited

This book is published by
Grosvenor House Publishing Ltd
Link House
140 The Broadway, Tolworth, Surrey, KT6 7HT.
www.grosvenorhousepublishing.co.uk

A CIP record for this book
is available from the British Library

ISBN 978-1-83615-083-1
eBook ISBN 978-1-83615-084-8

In loving memory of

BILL

Every love story is beautiful but ours is my favourite

For our children
Alison, David & Stephen
Grandchildren
Paul, Aaron, Ben, Stevie, Dannii, Robbie & Ryan
Great grandchildren
Olivia, Jorja, Ruby, Amelia and Zoey

Contents

Part Two

I was encouraged to write my story based on the experiences I encountered as a full-time carer for my husband as he succumbed to the dreaded disease that is dementia. It wasn't an easy journey but one that I was determined to see through until the end. It includes his life growing up in Belfast as the eldest of five children in a single parent family. His father had left Ireland when he was just 8 years old and two weeks before his youngest child was born. He never returned and very rarely supported them and so the family suffered many hardships. We met when our paths crossed at the time Bill moved to England, aged 21, to find work and spent the next 63 years of our life together.

Author: Rita Beggins

Acknowledgements

I thank my family for their love and belief in my ability to write my story.

My niece Claire Bullen for proof reading and editing my manuscript. Without her support and encouragement, I would not have had the confidence to self-publish this book.

Jasmine Damaris of Grosvenor House Publishing for guiding me through the process.

PROLOGUE

From the day of his passing on Wednesday 19th November 2018 at 12.15pm until his funeral on Friday 7th December, it was like living in a bad dream. Where do I go from here? After so many years together, I felt lost, I just couldn't visualise a life without him. He was my life.

In one of his letters from long ago, in the first year of our courtship, he said that he wanted to spend the rest of his life with me and for us to be lifelong partners and the feeling was mutual. It wasn't meant to be like this, we were meant to be together for always; he got his wish and did get to spend the rest of his life with me but where did that leave me, alone without my soulmate beside me. I expected us to be together forever; it had never entered my head that one day I would be left alone but being realistic, although it would be the perfect scenario to grow old together and leave this earth together, it would be an unlikely one. Although it's not the parting that I would have chosen, I am glad that I was the one that was left behind and that I had the opportunity and privilege of caring for him right to the end. I felt I owed it to him as he had cared for me for almost 63 years and I loved him with all my heart.

The loneliness of living with dementia was so different to the loneliness I felt afterwards. At least with dementia he was still physically with me, I could see him and give him comfort when he needed it. I could sit beside him and talk to him albeit he couldn't always respond and have a meaningful conversation with me, but it helped and passed the time as I cared for him. Once in bed, he was usually asleep by 9.30pm and I would be curled up on the settee alone and exhausted and I don't mind admitting it was tough and many times the tears would flow. As I look back on those times now, I think that was when I started to grieve. I just wanted to make life a little easier for him but each day he deteriorated just a little more and I felt helpless. There was nothing I could do to stop his decline. I knew in my heart that I was slowly losing him. It was the toughest thing that I have ever had to cope with.

After his passing and when the family had all returned to work and their everyday lives, the house felt so empty and the loneliness at times was unbearable. When the weather permitted, I spent a lot of time walking around the garden that he loved and where every day I felt his presence close to me. I still expected to hear his voice calling me and I talked to his photograph all the time just as if he was right there in the room with me. Every day I just went through the motions of day to day living not really taking anything in or even wanting to. I found it hard to accept that I was never going to see him again, maybe it had all been a bad dream and I would wake up and he would be there, smiling at me with that smile that lit up his whole face and shone in his eyes. The look that said he loved me, the look that needed no words.

I would have the television on just to hear another voice in the room and I would listen to the music that we had loved and enjoyed together. So many beautiful memories. I made food for myself that I didn't really want to eat, a cup of tea just general everyday things; I felt I had to keep going for the rest of the family even though they are all adults. I didn't want to burden them with my sadness and grief, they had their own grief to deal with and so I felt I needed to be strong for them.

There was such a big void in my life and I don't think the ache in my heart will ever go away but I felt each day was becoming just a little easier or so I thought until one day, several months later, I was sitting in the conservatory with a cup of coffee just thumbing through a magazine but when I lifted my hand to touch my face, I felt the tears streaming down my cheek. Apart from the day he had passed I had shed no tears not even at his funeral, I didn't want anyone to think that I didn't care but I just felt so numb with grief. I don't know what triggered off these tears but all of a sudden, I was overwhelmed and I felt my heart breaking. This was to happen to me several times over the following weeks and months, I could be at the sink washing up, doing the ironing or some other everyday mundane task, when the tears would suddenly begin to flow. I thought they would never stop.

I had lost my parents many years before but I had never felt grief quite like this. Maybe that was because, when my parents died, I had a young family and although devastated, I had my children to care for and so it kept me occupied and helped me to cope with that loss. This loss was so different, I felt so alone even though I had the support of my children, grandchildren and other family members who were all there for me and lived close by. I knew I only had to lift the phone and one of them would be there for me but this was something I had to get through on my own. I had to learn to cope and to move on to a life without him in it. That is what he would have wanted for me and so that is what I have to do for him. We had a good life together raising our family and he has left me with a lifetime of memories of the happy times we shared. When I am feeling sad and lonely, I listen to our music and I read his letters from long ago. I go through the many photographs that

I have and as I take a trip down memory lane, he is always there waiting for me.

To fully understand the man that I had loved, married and lost after more than 63 years together to the cruel disease that is dementia, I feel I need to tell you his story as he told it to me and of our life together.

PART ONE

1

BILL – HIS EARLY LIFE
IN NORTHERN IRELAND

Bill was a Belfast man who was born into a Catholic family in Northern Ireland on the 18th of August 1934. He was a premature baby and born at home, as were most babies back then. As he was not expected to survive the night, he was wrapped in a shawl and gently laid in a shoe box which was placed close to the fire to keep him warm. He was baptised William John by the midwife which was a common occurrence in the circumstances. Prayers that were said throughout the night were answered and his mother was overjoyed when her first born, who proved himself to be a fighter, survived the next 24 hours and went on to thrive. He was named after his maternal grandfather who had been baptised and brought up as a Protestant. His family were members of the Orange Order and disowned him when he started seeing a Catholic girl. Although he eventually married her in the Church of Ireland, his family would cross the street rather than pass on the same side of the road as him. They never spoke to him again.

Bill was the eldest of five children and life was tough for him growing up in poor times in a city that had very little work for its menfolk. When he was 8 years of age, his father left the family home with the intention of finding work elsewhere and just two weeks before his fifth child was born. He never returned to Ireland or indeed to his family

1

and so he never ever saw his youngest child. As she grew up, Bill looked out for her and became a father figure to her. As a baby he would nurse her and feed her and was the only one who could get her to settle. As young as he was, he became the man of the house, helping his mother with the younger children so that she could find work to feed them. He would help the milkman with his round by collecting the empty bottles from doorsteps before he went to school in the mornings and the few pennies that he earned he gave to his mother so that she could buy milk for the new baby.

There weren't benefits and very little help in those days and only on a rare occasion did his mother receive any sort of child support from her husband for their children. Family allowance, as it used to be called, didn't start until August 1946 and this was1942. Even then it was not payable for the first child but 5/-d. per week (25p) in today's money, was paid for the second and each subsequent child and so it was left to her to find work to provide for them. Her only income was what little she earned from scrubbing floors. Her husband was living in England and would send letters on the odd occasion, pouring out his love for her and the family they had had together. He told her how much he was missing them all and couldn't wait until he was able to come home to see the new baby that had been born just two weeks after he had left, whilst at the same time making excuses as to why he could send no money. It would be because he had a cold and was unable to work, he had hurt his leg and needed a walking stick or had got something in his eye and needed to wear an eye patch. They were such pathetic letters from a man whose only thought appeared to be for himself. I have read these letters; they are in my possession and so I know these stories to be true. There was always some

2

lame excuse. I wonder whether he ever gave a thought to how difficult life was for his wife who was left to raise their children as a single parent. He would ask after the children and continually requested photos of them and wanted his three sons to have boxing lessons; a cousin was Northern Ireland's world champion boxer, Rinty Monaghan. There was no thought of where the money was coming from to pay for photographs. People didn't have cameras back then and if you could afford them, photographs were usually taken in a studio or often by a street photographer. He said that he would buy them the boxing gloves but how could she be expected to pay for the lessons when there was little enough money to feed them with. It didn't help either that food was rationed due to the war. The Authorities (the NSPCC back then) did try to trace him for maintenance money from time to time but he would change his name and move on if he got wind of anyone looking for him and so the family continued to struggle and make the best of what little they had.

Bill had so much to contend with in his young life, his father leaving the family home at a time when Britain was at war with Germany. Having to look after the younger children so that his mother could work to put food on the table and then being evacuated to the country together with his younger brothers and sisters, away from the bombing of the city when the air raids started, which was scary and unsettling for the family. He had developed a stutter which would cause him so many problems throughout his early years. His maternal grandfather who he had been named after, did his best to help him and so that when he was sent to the shop for errands, he would write notes for him to hand over to avoid him having to speak to the shopkeeper and that way he only had to answer with a 'yes' or 'no'.

Life at school was difficult for him and the stuttering became worse and for this he was bullied and picked on by some of his teachers, the Christian Brothers; not very Christian of them. When it was his turn to stand up in front of the class to read, he knew that the moment he began to stutter he would be beaten and because of this he started to play truant on the days that he had one particular teacher that would delight in humiliating him. Over a period of twelve months, he missed school less than half a dozen times but it was enough for the Catholic Church, who ran the school, to bring his mother before the authorities. Rules in Ireland were very strict back then and the Church had a big say in the rules and regulations and indeed into family life. It was decided that, as his mother was trying to raise five children alone with no father in the home, that it would be better for Bill and in his best interests, to spend the final 3 years of his school life in a Boy's Home. No-one had taken into consideration what he had had to cope with in his young life or how that might have affected him.

I can only imagine how he must have felt at being separated from his mother and siblings. He must have been terrified. It was harsh treatment for a boy, just 11 years old, who found himself in this position through no fault of his own but due to the family's circumstances. His mother must have been heartbroken that this should happen to her eldest child who had been such a help to her in caring for his siblings while she worked. His father had a lot to answer for. I wonder did he ever think of his wife and the children he had left behind and how they were managing? As a parent myself, I cannot imagine how anyone could possibly leave their home and family and never return, not even to see their young children again.

Bill had been in the Home for a year when he was told that his maternal grandmother had died. She had always been there for him in his early years and he was close to her. She would take him everywhere with her when he was a small boy and so he had more heartbreak to contend with and no one to comfort him. It wasn't the first time he had buried his head in the pillow as the tears flowed.

One of his duties at the Home, apart from his lessons, was to help in the gardens and he was encouraged by one kind Brother who took him under his wing and taught him the basics of gardening. Gardening was to become his great love and something he enjoyed and never grew tired of. He loved the work, learnt a lot and many years later it was, for him, the start of a career in horticulture.

Once a week, the boys were taken to the Broadway Cinema for the Saturday matinee and could be seen walking 2 x 2 along the street. A second cousin of Bills, that I came into contact with through my Ancestry research into his family history, told me that he and his brother who were of a similar age, used to wait for the boys coming down the street and would jump on the end of the line so that they could get into the cinema and see the film for free.

One morning Bill was excused from his lessons and told to go home as his mother needed him. The family had had to leave the home they were living in, some time before, as there was no longer money for rent as well as food and so they were living with their paternal grandmother, their uncle, who was their father's younger brother and his young daughter. The uncle was about to reconcile with his estranged wife but she wouldn't move into the house unless his sister-in-law and her children moved out but where could they go. Without sufficient funds there was nowhere. To facilitate this, the grandmother, without her daughter-in-law's knowledge and with the help of the nuns she worked for, arranged for the children to be moved into a Children's Home and their mother left to fend for herself. Bill, who was just a child himself, was needed to help with that move.

When the few possessions they had were loaded onto a handcart, they headed, with his younger brothers and sisters to the children's home where they were to stay. The youngest child was just 4 years old and the eldest 11. What a sad sight that must have been; a young homeless mother trudging along the street with her few belongings on a handcart and followed by her five bewildered children. She was devastated at having to say goodbye to them and to hearing their cries as she walked away. She had already been parted from her eldest son for the past couple of years and now, she was to lose the rest of her young family. She must have wondered what she had done to deserve such harsh treatment and what sort of a so-called Christian family she had married into. She was heartbroken and for Bill to see her so distressed was a memory he never forgot throughout his life. He had already experienced being separated from his family and now he was seeing his siblings going through the same trauma and he knew just what that was like. How cruel for a grandmother to do this to her own flesh and blood. Surely, there must have been some other way to handle the situation. Could they not have sat down around a table and tried to find a solution that benefitted them all. Seeing how her eldest son had treated his family it could be said that the apple never falls far from the tree. Bill understandably never ever forgave his father or his grandmother for the way the family were treated. He made a vow to himself that when he grew up, if he had a family, they would always be his top priority and if necessary, he would work his fingers to the bone to provide for them.

It was fortunate for them that his grandfather who was living alone after the death of his wife, in a very small flat above a greengrocers' shop, heard what had happened. He told his daughter to go and fetch her children from the Home and to bring them back to live with him. Because of his actions they were only in the Home for two nights. He had very little to offer them but could not bear to see his grandchildren taken into care and parted from their mother. It's hard to imagine how they would have suffered or how it would have affected their future lives had their grandfather not stepped in to provide a home for them. As small and as overcrowded as it was, they were to live with him for the rest of his life. At least they were all together, apart from Bill, as a family and no-one was ever going to split them up again.

The boys at the Home were allowed out once a month for a weekend to visit their families provided they had all behaved themselves. If just one boy had stepped out of line, then none of the boys were allowed home visits and so they were all punished. This happened more often than not and so during his years there, Bill lost the bond he had had growing up with his siblings resulting in him feeling an outcast, at times, within his own family for many years to come.

2

THE GREEN GLENS OF ANTRIM – HIS FIRST EVER HOLIDAY

There was a big old house situated in the Glens of Antrim near to the village of Cushendall and in the Vale of Glenariff, it was where the boys from the Home were taken each summer for a two-week holiday. Never ever having had a holiday before, Bill fell in love with the beautiful area he found himself in. The house was surrounded by gardens and once again he found himself helping with the upkeep. They walked everywhere through the Glens and the boys were often to be seen walking down the lane to the beach, in the care of one of the Brothers and with their towels rolled up and tucked under their arm. For him it was respite from what was an unhappy period in his life. For the 3 years he was in the Home it was something he could look forward to each summer. Over the years he was to return to the area many times and the Vale of Glenariff always held a special place in his heart.

When the time came for him to leave the Home, he was 14 years old, the school leaving age at that time and he needed to find employment. This is when his paternal grandmother, who was a very religious woman, came back onto the scene. She had obtained work for him tending the garden in the local Convent. As there was no other work available, he had no choice but to take the job and hoped what little he earned would make life just a little easier for his mother. He had left school with no qualifications so there were not many opportunities open to him. He was badly paid and the Nuns wanted their pound of flesh. After a year he found out that they were paying him well below the going rate for the work he was doing and so he decided to ask for a rise. A big mistake; that didn't go down very well with the Mother Superior and she threatened him with his grandmother. The cheek of him, how dare he ask for more money when they had been kind enough to offer him work. When his grandmother found out he got a clip round the ear for being so bold. Needless to say, he left and found other menial work.

We had many a laugh over the years when he would tell our children, when they were looking for money, what his wage was in his first job. It was pre-decimalisation and his weekly wage was £2. 2s. 1½d which he would hand over to his mother at the end of each week. She kept the £2 for housekeeping and would hand him back the 2s. 1½ (pronounced, two and three halfpence) his pocket money for the week. She also gave him a Park Drive cigarette every morning as he left for work. This was long before there were any health concerns related to smoking. We all laughed so much when he said how one evening, he was going out with his mates and feeling very grown up and one of the boys, asked if he could have another cigarette to go out with. Her reply was "run away on wee boy, what did you do with the one I gave you this morning." We loved to hear his stories of growing up in Belfast, some sad and some so funny at that way he would tell them to us. His life growing up was so different to my early years. We didn't have much but what we did have were two loving parents that always put us first. Our children couldn't relate to his childhood years at all. Life was so different for them and because of his work ethic they wanted for very little.

He loved going to the cinema and his other passion was ballroom dancing. Saturday nights were taken up with dancing at the Plaza Ballroom in Belfast where he and his mates would check out the local female talent. A typical pastime at that time for teenage boys with raging hormones. He took ballroom dancing lessons and won his bronze medal at the age of 16.

As he grew up, he could see no future for himself in Belfast, as being a Catholic there weren't the job opportunities and so he made the decision, when he was 18 years old, to leave his hometown and join the Royal Airforce. Once again, he was to be separated from his family. He spent two years in the RAF Regiment starting his service at RAF Bridgenorth, a recruit training station in Shropshire where he did his initial 8 weeks training. Although he enjoyed the experience and the two years of his life whilst in the service, both travelling around the country and the time he spent overseas in Germany, he looked forward to returning to his homeland and his family in Ireland. He was hoping that work opportunities had improved whilst he had been away and that he would finally be able to get a decent job and to settle down; he had missed out so much on family life. Unfortunately, this was not the case and within a few weeks he made the decision, in August 1955, to move to London where there were more opportunities for permanent work and with a better rate of pay.

It must have been daunting for him, moving to a big city in another country, not knowing anyone and being completely alone. However, he had left Belfast once before and he could do it again. He was so desperate to make something of himself and to improve his prospects and his life.

He felt that he could only do that by making a fresh start in a new country and so he started out, at just 21 years of age, on what was to become a new life for him. Some of the money he had received on leaving the RAF he had put to one side to tide him over until he was settled.

3

NEW BEGINNINGS – LONDON, ENGLAND

On his arrival in London, he signed up for any temporary work that was available and his first job was at the Nuffield Centre, an ex-service men's club that was off Trafalgar Square where he took a job as a kitchen porter. He had found accommodation in a big old house, in the Stamford Hill area of North London, that was let out into rooms. The only vacancy was a single bed-sit in the attic. It was very basic accommodation with no carpets or comforts and just the bare necessities. A single toilet and bathroom, two floors below, were shared with the other tenants. He wasn't used to luxuries, so he was more than happy to have found a job, to have a roof over his head and a bed to sleep in. It was a very lonely life for him as he didn't know anyone in London and the only people that he met were the people he worked with and they went home to their families at the end of the working day. Also doing temporary work he wasn't in any one job long enough to make friends. The other tenants, where he lived, worked different hours so he didn't have much contact with them either and they tended to keep themselves to themselves.

Over the following weeks and months, he took the opportunity of finding his way around London. He visited the many tourist sites, armed with his battered 'Box Brownie' camera that despite being held together with Sellotape, he treasured. He wanted to take photos that he could send home to his family and to show them the area where he was to settle.

Coming from a close-knit family I can't begin to imagine what life was like for him at that time. Looking back now I can understand why his one ambition was to secure permanent employment and to settle down with a family of his own. He had missed out so much on a stable family life.

4

THE FIRST TIME EVER
I SAW YOUR FACE

Something happened the day when I first met him and even now, all these years later, I really can't explain the feeling I had. It was certainly a WOW! moment. Was it a woman's intuition or is there really such a thing as love at first sight? I just knew that the moment our eyes met that he was special and that I wanted to get to know him. I was 17 years old and although I had had a couple of boyfriends, they were nothing serious and were more friends that just happened to be boys than anything else. This was something different though and a feeling I had not experienced before.

It was January 1956 and I was working for the John Lewis Partnership in their offices in Bolsover Street which was half-way between Oxford Circus and Regents Park Underground Stations. I had started work with the company on leaving school the year before. I worked on the fourth floor as a shorthand-typist in the Records Office of the Department of the Directorate of Building which was spread over the top two floors. The other floors of the building were taken up with the Buying Offices. The Directorate of Building housed the Architects, Quantity Surveyors, Heating & Ventilating and Electrical Engineers. Apart from the secretaries of each department, who tended to be older women and mostly in their thirties; positively ancient in my eyes back in those days, there was only one other young girl, Maria, a filing clerk that worked with me. Maria had been born in England to an Italian family who had old fashioned values and were very protective of her. She had been told that if a boy kissed her, she would get pregnant and to steer clear of them. Each of the sections had an apprentice so there was no shortage of boys of a similar age and we tended to hang out together. Maria always stayed close by my side. We would meet up for tea breaks and would often take a walk to Regents Park in our lunch hour if the weather was fine.

I had been off sick for a couple of weeks with laryngitis and returned to work towards the end of January. I arrived on my first morning back and as usual stopped to pick up the mail from the pigeon-holes on the ground floor. As I turned around, I stopped dead in my tracks, he was just standing there watching me and as I looked up and our eyes met, he smiled and winked at me. He had dark wavy hair, the bluest of eyes and just the hint of a dimple. My heart felt like it was doing somersaults and I must have blushed from head to toe; I got all flustered and quickly turned to get into the lift but he was there before me and opening the door. I pressed the button to take me up to the fourth floor and ready to start my day's work but I couldn't get him out of my head all morning; that smile and those eyes, what a combination! I hadn't seen him around before, so I guessed he was a visitor.

When I went for my tea break that morning, I was sitting chatting to some of the apprentices as usual when I had the feeling that I was being watched. As I looked up, there he was again, two tables away, sitting alone and staring straight at me. He winked again and smiled as our eyes met. It was one of those moments when you look into someone's eyes and you just know. This was something that had never happened to me before and I wasn't quite sure what to do and was feeling a little embarrassed. Had anyone else noticed this connection between us as our eyes met? I just felt as if everyone was looking at me. I quickly drank my coffee; made my excuses to the others I was with and got up to leave. The canteen was in the basement and so I made my way to the lift. When it arrived, I went to open the door but a hand came across and opened it for me, he had followed me out. Instead of getting off at the ground floor, he took the lift straight up to the fourth floor which gave him time to ask my name and introduce himself. He had been working as a temporary assistant to the Concierge which involved sorting the mail for the various departments and dealing with outgoing post and stationery. As I got out of the lift, he looked at me, smiled, winked again and said, 'see you around.' That wicked wink, those blue eyes and that smile were to be my downfall. I was hooked.

He had been working in the building for three weeks and as I had just returned to work after being off sick it explained why I had not seen him before. From then on, wherever I went in the building he would suddenly appear. Every morning he was there when I arrived, he would hand the mail to me and open the door of the lift. I was quite shy until I got to know someone and so I felt myself blushing from head to toe every time I saw him. There was certainly a big attraction between us and it was quite obvious he felt it too.

I used to work one Saturday morning in every four and that Saturday it was my turn to work. My boss and Maria were both off, so I was in the office on my own. I hadn't seen him when I arrived that morning, so I presumed that he was also off, until the phone rang. It was him and he asked me if I would go out with him that evening. One half of me wanted to jump for joy and say yes but I felt I didn't really know him that well, after all we had only met 5 days before and back then girls rarely said yes the first time they were asked out on a date (well nice girls didn't anyway). It wasn't unusual for us to play hard to get and the usual excuse we gave was "I'm washing my hair tonight". He asked had I a boyfriend that I was going out with and I replied 'no'. I said I lived too far away to go home to Morden, get changed and then travel back up to London again. Not to be put off he said, "well what about next week then," he was very persistent and asked me every day until I agreed to a date after work on the following Thursday 9th February 1956. I was excited and nervous all at the same time, what if I didn't meet up to his expectations and he didn't like me?

That week he took every opportunity to stop and chat with me, always timed his tea breaks to coincide with mine and would usually come to sit with me. Thursday came round quickly enough and when I finished work, he was waiting for me as I stepped out of the lift. We stopped for a coffee in a little coffee shop on the corner which, incidentally, is still a coffee shop all these years later. The office building however has now been turned into luxury apartments. We chatted non-stop, each of us asking questions of the other and I soon felt at ease in his company. He was so easy to talk to and that was one thing we always had in common, we could talk about anything and everything and it was like that throughout our life together. I noticed that he had a bit of an accent and thought maybe he came from somewhere in the north of England. Back then, in the area where I grew up, we didn't really come across different accents or people from other countries but were just aware that people spoke slightly differently depending on which part of the country they came from and so I was surprised when he told me he was

Irish and came from Northern Ireland. Believe it or not I hadn't really heard an Irish accent before or not that I was aware of and he never did have a very strong accent anyway. So that's where those gorgeous blue eyes came from. He smiled with his eyes and the song 'When Irish Eyes Are Smiling' described him perfectly.

He took my hand as we walked down Regent Street towards the London Pavillion at Piccadilly Circus, where we saw the film, 'Rebel Without A Cause' starring James Dean and Natalie Wood. It was one of the big films of the day. Many years later and after we were married, we would often watch a video of the film when the anniversary of that first date came around. A date we never forgot and even now I still remember the occasion. As we left the cinema, we walked down to Leicester Square and stopped for a coffee and a sandwich. We just never stopped talking, we wanted to know everything there was to know about each other as we walked down to Trafalgar Square, across Hungerford Foot Bridge and along the South Bank to Waterloo Station where I could get the train home. Over the next three years it was a walk we were to do many times after our nights out in London.

He told me all about his family and asked me about mine, what music I liked, did I like dancing. He said he missed going to the dances at the Plaza ballroom when he had lived in Belfast. Back in the 50s we all did ballroom dancing but rock and roll had also just arrived and I was a big fan. He told me his favourite record was Bob Manning singing 'The Nearness of You' not only had I not heard of the American singer I had never heard of the song either. That was put right on our second date, which was just a few days later, when he turned up with a card and a present for me. It was a

78rpm recording of his favourite song which just happened to be a very romantic one. It was Valentine's Day and this 17-year-old girl was smitten.

When we arrived at the station, I was looking at the board for the times of trains and told him that my train was due to leave in 10 minutes and that I needed to get to the platform otherwise I would miss my connection for the last train from Wimbledon. He decided to get a platform ticket so that he could see me onto the train, he lived an hour's journey in the opposite direction. He was talking to me through the open window of the train but as the guard blew the whistle, he suddenly opened the door and jumped in, no automatic doors back then. He didn't want to leave me there and had decided to go as far as Wimbledon where I changed trains onto the local line. We had the carriage to ourselves and so he put his arm around me and gave me that first kiss as we snuggled up together. We just seemed to click right from that first moment when our eyes met and we both knew that this would be the first of many dates. Many times, when he bought a platform ticket, he would jump onto the train at the last minute and travel to Wimbledon with me. Back then a platform ticket cost 1d. (that was an old penny) so it was a cheap ride from Waterloo to Wimbledon and return. I was very surprised to find that platform tickets are still available today at a cost of 10p but are mainly used by train spotters at main line stations and are only valid for an hour. All train carriages were made up of single compartments back then and so tickets were only checked as you got on or off the train whereas now the guard can walk through the length of the train checking tickets. If you went through the barrier with a platform ticket it was assumed that you had either been saying goodbye to someone on the train or you were meeting someone off the train.

We would usually go out after work a couple of times during the week. Very often we would just walk down to Leicester Square and stop for a coffee and for Bill it was always a salt beef sandwich, his favourite filling. From there we would carry onto Trafalgar Square for our usual walk to Waterloo crossing the Thames via Hungerford Bridge over to the South Bank where we would sit on a bench together overlooking the river until it was time to head to the station for my train home. We would also see each other at the weekend. I could get up to London easy enough, at no extra cost, as I had a weekly season ticket. We usually met in London as it was the half-way point between our homes and there was such a lot to see and do there. London is a city you never grow tired of. We would go to the pictures from time to time but it was expensive and wages were low, so we would spend our dates, like most couples of that time, visiting the many parks in London or walking along the embankment. We could often be seen snuggled up together on a park bench somewhere. This was to be the start of many happy years together. He was now settled in a new country with a job albeit a temporary one, a place to live and now he had a girlfriend. The way he saw it, his life could only get better and he had high hopes for his future.

John Lewis had quite a social side and there were regular dances held in one or other of their branches. We attended dances at the John Barnes branch in Finchley Road and sometimes Peter Jones in Sloane Square. Once a year in March they held a Summer Ball at the Albert Hall and we had tickets to go. I told my parents that it didn't finish until midnight but that someone would be seeing me home so not to worry. We were too late for the train home from Waterloo and so we got the tube to Morden which was the end of the Northern Line. As the last bus had already left, we then had half an hour's walk to my house from there. We said goodnight as he left and made his way to our local station to wait for a train that would take him to Wimbledon and then onto Waterloo for his journey home to North London. My dad would usually go to bed if I was out but my mum always waited up until I was home. She saw Bill turn and wave to me and asked who he was and how he was going to get home. I said he was getting the milk train that went through at 2.30 every morning and explained that he lived the other side of London, so he had quite a long journey ahead of him. The fact that he saw me home to the door and knowing he lived such a distance away, scored him brownie points and I was told to invite him to tea the following Sunday so that my parents could meet him. They were already aware that I had been seeing someone, so I guess they needed to check him out. That's just how things were done back then. I can just imagine the reaction a 17-year-old girl would have today if they were told to invite a boyfriend home to Sunday tea to be checked out by the parents. I'm sure my grandchildren would have a chuckle reading this but life for us was so different back then and not one they could relate to at all. They have so much more freedom now.

5

MEETING THE PARENTS

Sunday came round soon enough and Bill was happy to be invited to meet my family. He got on well with them right from the start and loved Morden, the area where I lived. Compared to Stamford Hill it was like being in the country. Stamford Hill was a very busy, built-up area of North London with many nationalities living there. He soon became a regular visitor on Sundays and got on well with my dad. He would join him for a pint at the George Inn, my dad's local, while I helped at home with the lunch. I was so glad my parents liked him as I knew in my heart this was the real thing and that we would spend the rest of our lives together.

It soon became the norm for us to go out after work a couple of times during the week and now that Bill had met and been accepted by my family he would come over to Morden at weekends. We would usually go to the pictures locally as the tickets were much cheaper than the London cinemas or we would go to a dance at Wimbledon Palais or one of the other dance halls in the area. If we weren't dancing, we would be out walking in one of the local parks. As he lived so far away, he often stayed over on a Saturday night sleeping on our settee. Good news for my dad, he now had a regular drinking buddy for his Sunday lunch time pint. They got on very well together, he was like the father that Bill never had and he looked up to him.

Not many people had home phones back in the 1950s but being self-employed my dad had one for his work. Although the house where Bill lived had a phone, very rarely would he use it to ring me as it was in the hall and there was no privacy. He would go down to the nearest phone box armed with a handful of coppers and would ring me every evening that he didn't see me, he never missed a call. He would usually be chatting on the phone for 2-3 hours in fact most of the evening. Young love! From time to time during the call he would ask me to hold on while he put more coins in the box or because there was a queue of people outside waiting to use the phone. He would tell anyone waiting that he was on an emergency call and that there was another call box further down the road that they could use. The cheek of him. If I wasn't seeing him or speaking to him on the phone, then I was driving my family mad as I played my record of Bob Manning singing 'The Nearness of You' over and over. I often wonder what happened to that vinyl record as at the time I treasured it but I think I must have worn it out or possibly it is up in the loft and just maybe I should check it out especially as vinyl's are making a comeback.

Things were looking up for Bill, he no longer felt lonely, he had made some friends but more importantly we had each other and for the first time in a long time he felt settled, part of a family and that he belonged here. He also now had a permanent job working for the Parks Department of the L.C.C. (London County Council).

The one thing that disappointed him was that many weeks would go by with no word from his family in Ireland. He would write to them from time to time but rarely did he get an answer unless there was some problem and naturally, he missed them. Without telephones the only means of contact back then was by letter and corresponding takes time and effort. I think the bond they had as young children had been lost due to the 3 years that he had spent in the Boys Home and then in later years the 2 years he was away from home serving in the RAF. They no longer had anything in common and he felt they had grown apart but in fact as they were all younger than him, they were probably all finding their own way in life. He must have seemed more like a stranger to them. Although he would get homesick from time to time, especially at Christmas, he never ever regretted his move to London and looked on England as his adopted country. A country that had given him hope and expectations for his future.

It was just about 12 weeks after we first met and the weekend of my 18th birthday when I got a birthday surprise that I wasn't expecting. We had been invited to lunch, with my parents, to visit my mum's brother and his wife on the following Sunday. They lived in Dorking and so Bill was to get to know another branch of the family and another area of Surrey. After lunch, my Uncle George said there was a park nearby if we wanted to go out and take a walk. We jumped at the opportunity to be on our own and so we set off in search of the local park. We were sitting on a bench chatting when Bill suddenly proposed to me. It was completely out of the blue and not something I was expecting even though we both had a pretty good idea that we would be together for always but it still came as a surprise to be asked the actual question; after all we had only been together for such a short time. I was gobsmacked and couldn't speak and so the question was repeated. I just looked at him and said, "are you joking," he said "no, I'm quite serious." I jumped up and threw my arms around his neck as he hugged me. He said, "I take it that's a 'yes' then". I guess my instincts were right on that first day that we met, it was love at first sight and we really were meant to be together.

We were both excited and happy but thought it best to keep the news to ourselves for the time being as I guessed my parents would think it was far too soon and that we were too young to be in a serious relationship or at least I was and they might have stopped me seeing him. We didn't want anything to spoil what we had and so it was our secret but we made a commitment to each other on that day. Bill was 4 years older than me and just coming up to 22, whereas my mum and dad were 29 and 32 years when they had got married and my dad thought that was quite early enough but no way did we intend to wait that long. We were from a different generation and like every generation had different ideas to the generation before us and we just wanted to be together for always.

There was also another problem that had not come up before, Bill was Roman Catholic and I was Church of England and coming from Northern Ireland that could be a big problem and the cause of some family friction, more on his side than mine. God forbid his Granny should ever find out! It was not a problem in our eyes, especially as he was now living in England and he was in fact a lapsed Catholic. He had grown up in a community that was divided but here all communities were mixed and in fact we would not even know the religion of our neighbours. The divide in Northern Ireland was very hard for me to understand at that time as it was something I'd never experienced in my lifetime.

6

LOVE LETTERS STRAIGHT FROM YOUR HEART

Every year the family went on holiday to Golden Sands Holiday Camp which was in Hopton a few miles this side of Gt. Yarmouth. We had been the previous two years and we were usually joined by other family members. This year it had been booked as usual for the last week in July. We were not looking forward to being parted for a whole week but we promised to write to each other every day. The letters were filled with love and our plans for the future; we had so many dreams. We had seen scenes in a film of the Isle of Capri and thought what an amazing place that would be for a honeymoon one day but of course that was always beyond our wildest dreams. It was unheard of for the working classes to travel abroad for holidays back then, they could never afford it, not even a day trip to France would be on the agenda. However, that dream was often talked about over the years and it was always part of our long-term plan that maybe one day we would get to visit there but sadly that wasn't to be. It is on my bucket list to visit the island and the Amalfi coast and maybe one day I can make that trip for both of us but I am beginning to feel I am running out of time. Life is passing by so quickly.

Being more realistic we settled on the Lakes of Killarney but that's another story. Bill had said many times since we first met that he would like to take me to Ireland to show me the land of his birth. Unfortunately, that was something my dad would never agree to. Back then going on holiday with a boyfriend was most definitely out of the question. That just wasn't done and so the question would never even be asked. How different things are in today's world when young girls would be telling their parents they are off on holiday with a boyfriend or moving in with them and not even thinking of asking for permission. In later years we were the same with our own daughter and no way would she have been allowed to go off on holiday alone with a boy either.

In September 1956, Bill's mother was ill and in hospital and so he went back to Ireland. He expected to be away no longer than two weeks but in fact it was six weeks before his return. After the first couple of weeks when we wrote to each other every day, the letters from him started to dwindle and I was beginning to think he may have met someone else and that maybe he had decided to stay in Belfast. I wrote telling him how I felt and got a letter by return, saying that as he had had to stay longer than he had expected, his money was running out and so he needed to take on a temporary job to tied him over and to pay for his return travel. Wages were paid weekly, in cash, back then and working-class people didn't have access to bank accounts and there were no debit cards or credit cards. There was no-one else and he was missing me just as much as I was missing him. He promised he would be back as soon as he could. I couldn't wait to see him; it was the longest time we had been apart since we had first met. On the day of his return, I took the day off work and met him at Euston Station. As crowded as the station was, he was still able to lift me up in his arms for that first hug and kiss that we had waited so long for.

There were many letters between us over the following years when either I was on a family holiday, or he was on a visit to Ireland. His letters always ended the same way, 'I'll love you forever.'

7

TOO YOUNG

We hated these times apart and felt enough time had passed and so we decided it was time to tell my parents how we felt and that we wanted to get married. We were told we were too young or at least I was and that they wouldn't give consent until I was 21. Back then you couldn't get married without a parent's consent if you were under 21. However, they did agree we could get engaged, if we still felt the same way, the following year when I was 19. Although we were disappointed the answer was not unexpected but at least they had accepted that we were serious about our relationship and that he was to be part of my life.

We didn't want to wait and at one stage, we even talked about eloping to Gretna Green where you didn't need parental consent if you were under-age. We were young and in love but that would have been such a big step to take and I knew my parents would have been devastated, so we started saving for our engagement and felt that we had at least taken a step forward. It was hard especially on Bill as living in a bedsit in Stamford Hill, it was a lonely life for him with no family links close by and he was desperate for us to be together. We lived 2 hours journey from each other and although we spoke to each other every night, we could only meet up a couple of evenings during the week. We missed working together in the same building as he was now working elsewhere. We looked forward to the weekends when he would stay over at our house. I was lucky I had my family and friends close by.

It was about this time that I decided to apply for another job as a Secretary to a Director of a finance company in Regents Street which meant I was still working in the heart of the West End but had a more responsible job and earning more money. Bill started work early and finished early so he had time to go home and change after work and he would be waiting outside for me as I finished on the nights that we would go out together. We were both saving what money we could and so we would spend our evenings together walking in Regents Park, St. James's Park or along the South Bank of the Thames which was always a favourite walk for us.

His sister in Ireland was getting married the following Easter and as her eldest brother he was going home to give her away. When he returned less than a week later, one of his younger brothers was with him. There was no work for him in Ireland and so he wanted to try his luck in London too. He had no money and so Bill had to finance him until he could find work. That put our savings on the back burner for a while but I could understand why he wanted to help him. After all he had been in the same position himself just a couple of years before and it had turned out to be a good move for him and there were certainly a lot more opportunities in London than there were in Belfast. Although he eventually found work in the projection room at a local cinema, London wasn't for him, he was homesick and only stayed for a few months before returning home to Ireland.

We got engaged on the 15th October 1957 as I was now 19. My parents organised a party for our friends and relatives and we were another step closer to our planned life together although we still had to wait until I was 21, another 18 months away. We had provisionally chosen the month of

June 1959 for our wedding as that was the month my parents had got married and my mum was checking out halls for the reception. Unfortunately, things didn't turn out quite the way we had planned.

At the end of 1958 I discovered I was pregnant and I was dreading having to tell my parents but Bill, as always, was there for me and held my hand tightly as we told them together. As expected, they were not exactly jumping for joy at the situation and I was surprised that my dad seemed to take the news better than my mum did. Being the only girl in the family I think she was disappointed that there would be no big white wedding for her only daughter and I could understand how she felt. From a little girl I had always dreamed of having the fairy tale white wedding and gliding down the aisle on my father's arm but it was not to be and suddenly it no longer mattered anymore. What did matter however, I was to marry this amazing man that I had fallen in love with the moment that our eyes had first met. From early on in our relationship, all we ever wanted was to be together and although things were not quite as originally planned, we were happy and any obstacles that cropped up would be faced together.

To have married in white, under the circumstances, would have been frowned on by most people back in the 1950s. Just another situation that would be looked on so differently in today's world where a young girl could walk down the aisle, heavily pregnant in a full bridal white fitted gown and nobody would bat an eyelid.

My parents stood by us, they were fond of Bill and knew he would take good care of me and once they had got used to the situation were very supportive. Our planned wedding date was to be brought forward by three months but finances would no longer stretch to that honeymoon in Killarney or anywhere else for that matter. However, although our plans had to change, we were happy that at last we would be getting married. After all we had been together for 3 years and engaged for 14 months of them. Bill had lived alone in London throughout that time and it was a lonely life for him with no family support whereas, I lived at home with my family. He promised he would always love me and take care of me no matter what the future held for us and I knew that he was sincere, meant every word and that I would always be able to rely on him and trust him. He was looking forward to being able to settle down at last with his very own family to care for. The one thing he had always dreamed of and it meant a lot to him.

I don't think the problem of his religion had ever come up with my family and as he was so desperate for us to be together, he said it was not a problem for him to get married in the Church of England irrespective of what his family might think. He said it was his life and he would lead it how he wished and he was so desperate to be settled down with a family of his own. A Registry Office was definitely not an option for either of us and so we arranged an appointment with the Rector of St. Lawrence's Church in Morden where I had been baptised. When he was asked what Church, he worshiped at, he said that since moving to England he had not attended any of the churches in the Stamford Hill area and that in fact he was a lapsed Catholic. The Rector said he had no problem with marrying us as his own daughter had married someone of the Catholic faith but he did ask Bill if he had thought carefully about his decision. The answer was 'yes' and so it was agreed that it would be best to put us both down as living at the same address and therefore in the same Parish so that the banns only needed to be read out in one Church.

He wrote to his family to let them know the situation and that the wedding was being brought forward. The short notice and lack of funds no doubt prevented them from attending the wedding but as we never received any congratulations or wedding cards from any of them, I guess it had not occurred to them that the wedding would not be in a Catholic church and he was hurt at their reaction. They obviously weren't happy that he was to be married outside his faith and I learnt many years later that his younger sister, who was in her teens at the time, had said to her mother that she wanted to be a bridesmaid at our wedding. She was told that that couldn't happen as the wedding was to be in an English church and that they sang Protestant hymns.

Accommodation was not easy to find and with a baby on the way even less so. However, my dad knew of an elderly widow, who lived alone with her son, and had heard that she had two unfurnished rooms that she wanted to let. He had known her husband well when he was alive and so she was willing to rent the rooms to us but it meant sharing the bathroom and kitchen. It was quite common for newly married couples to rent rooms back then as it was rare for working-class people to be able to buy their own homes and they had to rely on Council accommodation becoming available. Not the start we had planned for and it was not ideal but we accepted it and it was close to my family home.

8

OUR LIFE TOGETHER

We were married on Friday 13th March 1959 with my family and close friends there to support us and a reception for family and friends was held at my parents' home. My mum and dad bought us a bedroom suite for a wedding present and money we had saved went on other furniture and things needed for our new home. We never got the honeymoon we had hoped for in Killarney but were more than happy to be starting out on our new life together. Not having a honeymoon at that time was not an issue for us, as long as we were together we were happy. Each week we would be out buying things and we got a real kick out of shopping for furniture for what was to be our first home together and couldn't wait to move in.

Bill looked forward to coming home each evening to a hot meal on the table and an evening watching television in the comfort of this our first home together. It was the first time he had enjoyed any sort of family life or home comforts since he had left Belfast almost four years earlier and had never had a television set before. Although it was just two rooms, we had everything that we needed, the furniture was new, had been chosen by the two of us and we had made it comfortable and cosy.

It was hard to believe that we were already making plans for the new baby we were expecting and although much earlier than planned, we were excited and happy that at last we were together and life was good for us. Bill could hardly believe his luck, he had gone from living in Belfast with no work prospects, no qualifications and no future to look forward to until he had moved to London. A move which he never regretted and which turned out for him, to be a wise decision. He now had a permanent job with prospects, a wife, a home although only two rooms and a baby on the way. It was what he had always dreamed of a family of his own to love and care for. He was determined that they would have the best possible life he could give them, that they would never want for anything and that he would always be there for them. It was a vow that he had made to himself all those years ago when he saw how his mother had suffered and struggled trying to raise her family as a single parent.

After 3 years of courtship, I guess we expected marriage to be all moonlight and roses but in reality, life isn't quite like that. After seeing each other 3-4 times a week we looked forward to married life and to being together 24 hours a day, 7 days a week but it was different and we had to get used to each other's moods and any annoying habits that we might not have been aware that we even had and so it was like getting to know each other all over again. It was different now because we had the worry of responsibilities that we didn't have in our courting days and we didn't know what life had in store for us and so you could say it was a bit of a wake-up call but we soon settled down and were happy.

The first 3 months were fine because there was just the two of us and we were all loved up. You could say it was the honeymoon period for us and being pregnant I was very much cossetted by him. He would get up in the middle of the night to fetch me an apple and to make the cucumber sandwich that I craved for. We soon settled down to married life and embraced all what that entailed. The main pressure however fell on Bill as I had now given up work and all the financial responsibility fell on him to provide for his new family.

9

A NEW ARRIVAL

It was the 28th May 1959 and my 21st birthday. I had an ante-natal appointment at the hospital, my ankles were swollen and blood pressure was very high, I was diagnosed with toxaemia (pre-eclampsia) and was to be admitted. I had to go home to get my things and return to check into the maternity ward for bed rest. When I left the hospital, my mum was waiting outside for me, she had wanted to catch me before I went home so that she could give me my card and birthday present, a gold bangle watch. I was worried and in need of some moral support, so I was more than pleased to see her there. When I told her that I had to come back again she reassured me as mothers do and came home with me to help me get my things together. No mobiles back then and there was no way I could get hold of Bill and so I had to leave a message for him to let him know what was happening and where I was. He arrived at the hospital in time for the start of visiting that evening. I was in a single ward and being alone was feeling nervous and so I was relieved to see him. He had what looked like a newspaper parcel tucked under his arm. He placed it on the bed, gave me a hug and then removed the paper to reveal a bouquet of red roses and a birthday card that had the words 'With love to my darling wife on her 21st birthday'. Back then no self-respecting Irishman would be seen walking along the street with a bunch of flowers. We laughed, it was probably the first time he had ever bought flowers for a girl and it was certainly the first time I had ever received any.

My blood pressure was being checked constantly as it was still very high and I was told I would have to stay in hospital until the birth. Two weeks later as there was no improvement, they were going to induce the baby on the following Monday. I had absolutely no idea what that entailed and I wasn't enlightened and so was pleased that I went into labour naturally on the Sunday afternoon. By this time, I was sharing a small ward with another lady who was quite a bit older than me. She was 52 and had grown up sons. Her husband had called an ambulance because she was suffering from severe stomach cramps. On arrival at the hospital, she was examined and found to be in an advanced stage of labour and close to giving birth. What a shock it was for them, they had absolutely no idea that she was pregnant and thought she was going through the menopause. It was her second marriage, her new husband had no children and so he was absolutely delighted when they welcomed, what was to be her first daughter. Obviously, they were not prepared for welcoming a new baby into their household and didn't even have as much as a pack of nappies or a tin of baby powder.

Later that afternoon I started having the odd stomach pain and was feeling uncomfortable. I was so naive and put it down to the punnet of strawberries that I had scoffed earlier in the day. When a nurse came in that afternoon to check on us, Anne, the lady in the next bed mentioned that I had been having some pains. On examination I was told I was in labour and would be moved up to the labour ward.

Hospital visiting back then was 7.00-8.00 each evening with no other visiting during the day and only one visitor allowed which was usually the husband. When Bill arrived, he was told that I was in the labour ward and was given directions where to find me. So anxious was he to get there he fell up the stairs and bruised both his knees. It was a teaching hospital and so I was constantly being examined by nurses and medical students and so when he came into the ward, masked and all gowned up I didn't recognise him and had had enough of being prodded about, I thought he was just another medical student. I was so relieved when I caught sight of his smiling, blue eyes above the mask and realised who it was. It was comforting to have him there and he did his best to keep me calm.

Husbands never used to be allowed at the birth in those days but as I was so agitated, they let him stay. The labour ward was very busy and they needed someone to sit with me and hopefully to keep me quiet. Being my first pregnancy and with the addition of complications, I was so scared and had never known pain quite like this before. If this was what childbirth was like, then it was going to be a one-off as far as I was concerned as there certainly weren't going to be any more. The next thing I knew a doctor and midwife were in the room and I was being given an injection in my leg. Bill had been instructed on giving me the gas and air and I remember very little after that. I vaguely remembered seeing a baby before it was whisked away.

The next thing I remembered, I could hear someone talking about me, the room was fairly dark with just a small light on at the side of the bed. I was very drowsy but I heard them say "if she doesn't improve within the next half an hour then we need to send for her husband." Something was wrong; I turned my head and saw I was attached to the blood pressure monitor and a nurse was sitting in a chair beside me. I asked where my baby was as I didn't remember seeing her and thought the worse. I was told that she was fine and asleep in the nursery. I wasn't satisfied and had to see for myself that she was ok. As I was so distraught a nurse was sent to get her. They needed me to stay calm and to sleep but there was no way that was going to happen until I saw for myself that she was alright. Yes, it was a little girl that had been born earlier that evening Sunday 14th June, had weighed in at 5lb.4ozs. and two weeks before her due date. When the nurse brought her in, they put her in my arms, I held her for just a few moments but it was enough to settle me down. I fell in love with her at first sight, she was so tiny, so beautiful, so perfect and had blue eyes and red hair. We had already decided on names for a boy or a girl and had settled on Julia Helen for a girl. In the 1950s there were no scans and so the sex of a baby wasn't known until the birth and so came as a nice surprise. When the nurse asked me had we chosen a name, I just looked down at her and without thinking said Alison Rita; she didn't look like a Julia Helen.

She was taken back to the nursery; I calmed down and slept. The nurse had been taking my blood pressure every 15 minutes throughout the night but when I woke again, it was morning and the nurse had gone together with the blood pressure monitor. My blood pressure was still a little high but I was out of danger and was to be taken back to a ward and this time I had my baby in a crib beside me. I was in a fairly large, single ward on the ground floor with a window overlooking the gardens but I was confined to bed and the curtains were drawn to keep it cool from the rays of the sun. I couldn't take my eyes off our new baby and couldn't wait for Bill's visit that evening. He had a grin from ear to ear when he came in and this time the flowers weren't covered in newspaper, he was just so proud to be a new dad and wanted the world to know. He hugged me tight; he was over the moon to see me as I held our baby in my arms. We spent the hour just looking at her and letting her grip our fingers, we were mesmerised. I know we were biased but we thought she was the most beautiful baby that had ever been born. I was discharged 11 days later after spending 28 days in hospital. It was so good to get home to my own bed and for us to be back together again. I wanted to be hugged and loved, we had missed each other so much.

Alison was the first grandchild in my family and my parents were overjoyed to be grandparents, they adored her from the moment they first set eyes on her. I can always remember my dad saying to me, "she is so beautiful" as he looked down at the tiny baby that he was holding in his arms. Being his only daughter, he was inclined to spoil me at times and I could see I was going to have some competition for his affections.

A new little person had joined our family and life would never be quite the same again. Raising a family was going to be harder than I first thought. Instead of it being just the three of us, it seemed that everyone wanted a piece of our new baby. We never got a minute to ourselves. When I went round to my parents' home each day their main interest was the new baby that they just wanted to hold and pamper; they were besotted. When Bill came home from work, he couldn't wait to spend time nursing this baby girl who was gradually taking over our lives. I could understand how he felt he was a proud dad and he wanted his time with her too; after all I was with her all day. However, I was beginning to feel that I wasn't important anymore and that nobody was interested in me.

I missed going out to work and mixing with other people and the days were lonely with just a small baby for company. I missed Bill during the day but now found I had to share him when he came home. I was no longer the main one in his life. I felt I had no-one to talk to as a small baby that sleeps a good part of the day is no company whereas he was at work all day and able to mix and chat with others. I couldn't wait for her to fall asleep because once she was asleep, he would place her gently into her carry cot and I would get his full attention, he would give me a hug and ask how my day had been. What could I say, what had I done but look after a small baby, changed and fed her? I had nothing to talk about and at times I felt so lonely. I guess I was feeling a little bit neglected too as I had been the sole focus of his attention for three months and I wanted him all to myself again. Selfish I know but I missed that time that we had had together when it was just the two of us. I guess I also had a touch of baby blues and was feeling exhausted. She didn't settle well and never seemed satisfied after her feed. However, this little lady turned out to be a night owl and as soon as we got into bed at night then she would wake up after having had just a few hours' sleep and expected the same attention she had received during the day. She didn't think that night-time was for sleeping.

Our new landlady turned out to be difficult at times too and in all fairness, she was old and not used to having a baby in the house. I had the feeling she needed the money but not the tenants. Every morning she would say to me "I heard her again last night" and so the minute she cried we lifted her to keep her quiet, the worst thing we could have done as she soon learnt that this was the way to get our attention. We got very little sleep at night whereas this little minx got her shut eye during the day when she wasn't being cuddled and spoilt by her new grandparents and uncles. We longed for a proper home with our own front door and some privacy but most importantly the time to be alone together and adapt to being a family. Although we had our name on the Council housing list, we knew it would be a long wait. There had always been a housing shortage and very few working-class people were able to buy their own homes or rent privately.

The local Health Visitor called in to see how I was managing with the new baby. I was feeling a little tearful and I explained that she didn't settle well after feeding, that we were getting very little sleep at night and we were both tired. She suggested that I bring her to the baby clinic so that she could be weighed and checked over by the Doctor. She was fine but as she was not putting on weight, she was probably still hungry after she had been fed because I wasn't producing enough milk for her. It was suggested that she be gradually weaned onto the bottle. Once she started being bottle fed, she began to put on weight and I must say she was certainly a lot happier during the day but she was still very much a night owl and kept us awake at night. At least now I could catch up on my sleep when she slept during the day.

Having that first baby isn't easy, after going through the trauma of birth you are handed this little bundle of humanity who comes with absolutely no instructions at all and you are expected to know exactly what to do. In fact, I found even holding a tiny baby in my arms was quite frightening, especially after I had fed and changed her and she still continued to cry. You begin to wonder what you are doing wrong and it doesn't help that your hormones are all over the place. However, once her feeding was sorted and she was on the bottle I wasn't so tired or weepy and gradually felt more confident as I recovered from her birth. I took her to the clinic every week to be weighed and it gave me the opportunity of meeting other new mothers, making friends and comparing notes. Life began to get back to some sort of normality. I was the first of my friends to marry and have a baby and so they were all still working and I missed meeting up with them.

10

OUR FIRST TRIP TO IRELAND
AS A FAMILY

It was 1960 and Alison was 14 months old, when Bill took us to Ireland to meet his family for the first time. Having very little spare money, we had to travel by the cheapest route which was by coach from Euston to Heysham where we caught the overnight ferry to Belfast. It meant travelling for 24 hours and we could not afford a cabin and so we made ourselves as comfortable as possible in one of the lounges. It was a long, tiring journey and one I will never forget. As dawn broke, Bill wanted to go up onto the deck as the Heysham to Belfast ferry sailed into the Belfast Lough on this, the first visit to meet my in-laws with our baby daughter. I was feeling just a little nervous and apprehensive at meeting his family. Would they be prepared to forgive the fact that Bill had married outside of his faith. I had read some Irish history and knew of the religious bigotry that existed in some parts. As a Church of England Protestant who had married one of Belfast's Catholic sons would I be made to feel welcome?

The air was still and the water was calm as the ferry continued its journey along the Lough and the sun was just rising. I could see the green fields on either side with lights beginning to flicker in the houses. Smoke was rising from chimneys as the inhabitants prepared to face the new day. It was a wonderful sight and something stirred deep inside of me; it was a feeling of excitement and anticipation visiting this land of saints and scholars that I had read and heard so much about. This feeling of homecoming was felt strongly in Bill's heart who being brought up in Belfast was now returning for this, his first visit not only as a married man but as a new father, to the land of his birth and he was excited at the thought of seeing his family again after such a long time. When the ship docked, we were met by his brother who was waiting with a taxi to take us to the family home, in the Grosvenor Road.

We had travelled overnight on the ferry and arrived early in the morning in time for breakfast. It had been a long and tiring journey and I was not prepared for the feast that was put on the table before us; the full 'Ulster Fry' much the same as a full English but with just a few extras. However, I never did take to the buttermilk that was served and must say I prefer a cup of tea with my breakfast.

Alison was soon whisked away by her 17-year-old auntie, the young sister who Bill had nursed as a baby, to be shown off to her friends and all the neighbours, her little niece with the red hair and blue eyes of an Irish colleen. My worries were fading fast with the warmth of this welcome and from the very start I was made to feel a special part of this new family. His mother must have been so proud to see how well Bill had settled into his new life in England, that he had a permanent job with prospects and to see the love he had for his wife and young child. The family life that he had wanted for so long.

I enjoyed this first visit to Belfast and Bill couldn't wait to show me around his old haunts. Never short of a babysitter during our stay, I was soon whisked off for a couple of nights at the Plaza Ballroom. It was good to go out dancing again and having someone to baby sit for us. It had been a long time since we had a night out on our own and something I felt we needed. We had missed the nights out when we used to go to Wimbledon Palais before we were married. It felt like we were dating again. The holiday passed quickly and we were soon making the return journey back to our home in England. We both knew this would be the first of many holidays to Ireland.

It was about this time that our landlady showed her true colours and tried to cause trouble between us. It was no surprise really as we had seen the trouble that she continually caused between her other son and his wife who lived in the house next door. Bill had a couple of little gardening jobs which he would do after work, weather permitting, to earn extra money to make life a little easier for us. I never knew what time he would be home as there was no access to phones. If Bill came home earlier than expected and before I had returned home from my parents' house just a 10-minute walk away, she would say to him "she's not in yet, she should be home and have a dinner on the table for you after a hard day's work". If I had his dinner ready and he was home late because he was doing one of his gardening jobs then she would say to me, "he's late home again tonight, God only knows what he's getting up to. You can never trust a man" We knew exactly what she was like and knew she couldn't be trusted as we also caught her opening some of our letters. She would complain about the baby crying at night and it all added to the stress of the circumstances we found ourselves in. She did her best to cause trouble between us but she didn't succeed. Our love was too strong and so we ignored her but it was still stressful. What could we do; we had nowhere else to go and there was a shortage of rented accommodation and so we had to put up with the situation.

We were so desperate to have a home of our own so that we could live life how we wanted to. At times tempers would be frayed but arguments didn't last long as we always made up. We would argue about simple things, it might have been a tiring day and we would both be exhausted. Financial struggles didn't help and that is why Bill started doing the part time gardening jobs after work in the first place and it meant he would be late home sometimes. If I was emotional and tearful, he would hug me and tell me everything would be alright and not to worry. He was always very protective of me. I loved him so much and wanted everything to be perfect, but life isn't perfect. I felt guilty that I wasn't working and couldn't contribute to the finances. We were lucky that we had a love that many people never find in a lifetime and so we survived these difficult early years.

11

RETURN TO WORK

When Alison was two years old, she was offered a place at the local day nursery and we were delighted at this opportunity as spending her days with adults she was being spoilt and enjoying it. She needed to interact with other children of her own age and once she settled into the routine of the nursery school, she enjoyed it and became easier to handle without the tantrums. She liked singing and we would often sing to her, we taught her the Christmas carol 'Away in a Manger' as it was coming up to Christmas. When I picked her up from the nursery a few weeks later I was told that she was to be the star of the nativity play that they were putting on and would be singing the carol solo. A big ask for a two-year old I thought but we were really excited when the day came round for us to go and watch her. When it was time for her to sing her part, she was lifted onto a chair and one of the teachers started to play the piano with her introduction. She played the first few notes but silence and so she started again but our little star had stage fright and not a word came out of her mouth and so that was the end of her singing career. When we got home, we couldn't get her to shut up, she just would not stop singing the carol that she sang so well. She would stand up on a chair or on the table and entertain us.

Now that Alison was settled, I was able to go back to work and got a job as secretary to the Export Manager of a Knitwear Manufacturer in the New Kings Road in Putney. I would drop her off in the mornings at the nursery and my mum was only too delighted to be able to collect her in the afternoons, take her home and continue to spoil her until either Bill or I would pick her up when we returned from work that evening. With both of us working we were able to start saving again and financially life became just a little easier.

Just when things seemed to be going ok for us, Alison came home from nursery school with chicken pox and because she was so fretful, she stayed overnight with my parents until she recovered. I would go round early each morning, wake her up, get her dressed and give her breakfast before I went onto work. We both went back each evening and had a meal with the family before going home. She was getting too big to be in a cot, we had no room for a bed for her and our landlady was definitely not happy with a toddler in the house and so my parents suggested we carry on with the arrangement in the hope that our housing needs would be considered more urgent as we were separated from her. It meant that we were both only sleeping in the two rooms we were renting but we had no other option. Whenever things started to go well for us and we felt we were getting somewhere, something would always happen to spoil it and we would be back where we started. We never expected our married life to have so many problems which all revolved around our housing situation. We often wondered if it would ever get easier.

The situation was far from ideal travelling between our home and my parents' home even though they lived close by and they could see we weren't happy with the situation and so eventually they suggested we put our furniture into storage and move in with them until we got a proper home of our own. We were beginning to feel we were going even further backwards. The house only had two bedrooms and was overcrowded as my brother was still living at home but we managed, Alison had a small bed in my parents' room and we slept on a sofa bed downstairs. This meant we couldn't go to bed until everyone else had gone to bed and we had to get up before everyone else got up. It was stressful at times but at least we were together again as a family. It must have been just as difficult for my parents as their life was also being turned upside down and we felt guilty about that.

It was however, another 18 months before we were offered a flat in Tadworth. When we received the offer, we were over the moon, signed the agreement and paid two weeks rent in advance before we had even seen it; we were that desperate to have a proper home of our own with our own front door so that we could all be together. At the time I think if we had been offered a shed with a lock on the door, we would have accepted it. It was a nice, two-bedroom ground floor flat, in a block of six, with a small balcony and a flower bed to the front. Alison had her own room and what's more we no longer had to worry about disturbing anybody if she played up at night. It was time to set some ground rules for her.

12

A HOME OF OUR OWN

We loved the area; we were surrounded by countryside and it was just a short walk to Epsom Downs. Bill bought a moped to get him backwards and forwards to work as transport links, especially first thing in the morning weren't the best in our early years there. I was able to carry on working and would get the bus to Morden each morning dropping Alison off at the nursery on my way. However, one morning the Health Visitor was on the same bus and realised that we were no longer living in the area and so we lost the nursery place. It was yet another hurdle we had to overcome. However, one of the neighbours that I had got friendly with and who lived in one of the flats above, had a little boy of the same age who Alison used to play with. She offered to look after her until she started school the following year. It helped her out too as it meant she was able to earn a little extra to supplement her housekeeping money. In most cases mothers didn't work back then but stayed home to care for their children. Some would have office cleaning jobs in the evenings that they could do once their husbands were home and the kids were in bed. I had a portable typewriter and so I could also work from home typing addresses on 3000 envelopes a week. There were very few nursery places and all nurseries at that time were run by local Councils and you had to meet a certain criteria for a nursery place. Now that we had a proper home of our own this service was no longer available to us. Things were tough for everyone back then and so mums that were able, tended to help each other out with childcare.

We put the problems of the past four years behind us and looked forward to a new start to our family life together. This is what we had waited for, for so long and we were going to make the most of every moment. We were so happy to be together as a family at long last and to face up to whatever was in front of us without having to rely on anyone else. We had had a difficult start to our marriage due to the housing situation but it was time to put those early years behind us and to make a fresh start.

Bill loved gardening and so when we moved into our ground floor flat, which was our first real home together, we had a flower bed in the front which ran along the front and around the small balcony. It was springtime and so he set to work planting it up with summer bedding. It was full of colour from the many mesembryanthemums he had planted, and he was chuffed to get many compliments from our neighbours.

Having our own home, we were now able to have Bill's mum over for a visit. For him it was a big thing that he could afford to give his mother a break and the chance of a holiday and to show her what he had achieved but more importantly to be able to have some quality time with her. We took her to London to see the sights and she loved every minute of it. It was nice that she could meet my parents too. They all got on very well together and having her to stay with us I was able to form a relationship with her for the first time and we got on well. If Bill and I ever argued while she was there, she would always take my side. This was to be the first of many visits for her.

At long last we were now settled with a home of our own and with my extra earnings were able to add a few mod cons to the flat. We now had a twin-tub washing machine with spin dryer which was a belated wedding present from my younger brother, a fridge and a telephone so that I could now ring home for a chat with my mum and Alison could speak with her nanny. We were happy and settled in our new life and the following year were delighted that I was pregnant again and looked forward to a new addition to the family. This time it would be so different, especially now we had a home of our own and with the new baby we would start off as we meant to go on.

Our son David was born towards the latter end of 1965 and weighed in at 7lbs.14ozs. No complications with the pregnancy this time and I was home again within 7 days. Bill now had a son to carry on the family name, something I am sure all men hope for, he was really chuffed. He had a permanent grin on his face once again, was a good father, very much hands on and helped where he could. Thank goodness the new baby wasn't a night owl like his sister. In fact, he was the complete opposite and slept all the time. As the new baby shared her room she was happy to go to bed at night at a reasonable hour and at 6 years of age it was not before time I might add.

All Bill ever wanted in life was to better himself. Working for the L.C.C there was plenty of scope for advancement with on-the-job training and qualifications that were recognised everywhere. The L.C.C. were well known for the high quality of their training. He had started off as a parks labourer with no skills and was often called on to do park keeper duties which was the one job that he hated. He was always looking for opportunities for advancement and new job vacancies were always advertised internally and so he channelled his efforts through horticulture from planting up the flower beds in the park to propagating in the greenhouses.

When an opportunity arose, he transferred to arboriculture and with it an increase in salary. He loved working on trees and the job satisfaction that came with it. Once again, he started at the bottom as a tree feller's mate learning as much as he could and continued attending courses which resulted in him advancing to tree feller with his own gang of men. He never expected his men to do anything that he wouldn't do himself. If one of them complained that a particular job they had been asked to do couldn't be done then, without uttering a word, he would take his coat off, strap a safety harness on and with a chain saw in hand he would climb the ladder himself and show them how it was done. In doing this he gained their respect.

I can remember a day during a hot summer when David was just a baby in the pram, I met Alison from school and as it was so hot and we had no garden at the time, we went for a walk over to Epsom Downs and she was happy to be able to push the pram. We got an ice cream at the tea hut and sat down on the grass enjoying the sunshine. To my surprise I looked up and saw Bill coming along on his moped. Not the way he usually came home but he had finished early and had decided on the pretty route. When he saw us, he had a big grin on his face, he was so pleased to see us there and came over to join us. He got himself an ice cream and sat down on the grass beside us. He loved it if he could get home early so that he could spend time with the kids and help get them bathed and into bed.

As he sat down, he noticed I wasn't wearing stockings even though I was smartly dressed and he passed a comment about it. I said it was far too hot for stockings. When it was time for us to make our way home, he bent over and grabbed hold of my hand to pull me up. As he did so, he quietly said "don't you go out again without your stockings on." I laughed because in no way was he prudish and so I thought he was joking but he was quite serious. It was ok for him to see my bare legs, but he didn't want anyone else looking at them. They were for his eyes only. It was 1966, a different era and back then women usually dressed smartly and always wore dresses and stockings whenever they went out, even if it was just to do the shopping and I must say it was unusual for me to go out with bare legs unless of course we were on holiday. He liked me to look nice and normally never criticised what I wore or how I was dressed. It was a different generation and so different to how things are today; but I was happy with how things were back then. However, I must say my kids had a good laugh when I relayed this story to them recently. Can you imagine any man saying that to a woman nowadays? They would never get away with it but in all honesty, I liked how our life was back then.

It reminded me of something he wrote to me in one of his early letters, he was saying that he couldn't wait for us to get married but there was one thing he wanted to make clear to me and that was that he would wear the trousers in our house. Of course, he never did, I just let him think he did. Back then life was so different to what it is now. The man was the bread winner and was looked on as the head of the house while the woman was the home maker and looked after the children. If she did work, then what she earned was the jam that went on the bread that he put on the table. Although we worked as one, we both had our own roles. However, over the years I never did or bought anything for the house without his approval. We were partners and I felt he should have an input too but he was always happy to go along with whatever I wanted to do. He never denied me anything and always agreed with what I wanted. When we moved into our house, the garden was his domain and the house was mine and so, I more or less had carte blanche on what I did.

13

PROMOTION

I was so proud of him that day in 1966 when he came home and told me he had been further promoted to Supervisor of tree work covering parks and open spaces in the north of London including the likes of Holland Park, Kenwood, Parliament Hill and Hampstead Heath. It meant he would now be salaried staff and would be paid monthly. Although it was out of his area he was asked to also care for the trees along the South Bank. An area that had a special place in our hearts from the many walks of our courting days. The new job meant he would now be responsible for more than one gang of workers and would be required to travel across the north London area that he was responsible for and so a van went with the job. He now had 20 men working under him. He had come a long way from those early days as a park's labourer. As he didn't drive, driving lessons were arranged for him and so he obtained another skill.

This good news was followed by bad news. My parents were going on holiday to the holiday camp that we used to go to as a family before we were married. My mum desperately wanted us to join them with the children and offered to pay for us but Bill was booked to have his driving test that week and so we had to turn the offer down. The day before they were due to come home my dad rang to say that my mum had been taken ill and had been admitted to hospital with suspected appendicitis. An exploratory operation was performed on her the following day and when I rang the hospital asking how she was and whether she could be transferred to a hospital nearer to home I was told that wouldn't be necessary as she would be discharged within a couple of days and that it wasn't serious. My brother's friend who had a car offered to take him up to Yarmouth to see her and as David was just a baby and there was no one I could leave the children with I had asked Bill to go in my place especially as we had been told she would be discharged within a few days.

The first thing she asked Bill was how he had got on with his driving test. She was so thrilled that he had passed it and asked after the children. 3 days later I got a call to say that her condition had deteriorated and that the family needed to get to the hospital as soon as possible. My dad used to ring me each evening but on that particular day he rang me in the morning and so I was able to tell him about the change in her condition and that he needed to get to the hospital quickly. Fortunately, Bill hadn't left for work and was at home when I took the call and so he would take care of the children and I would travel up to Yarmouth with my two brothers. However, before we could leave, I had another call from my dad to say that he arrived at the hospital just as she passed. I had to break the news to my brothers. It was the 20th September 1966. Her death certificate showed the cause of death as Acute Pancreatitis. So much for being told her condition wasn't serious. Alison was 6 years old and David 10 months. It was such a shock, I was devastated, she had been such a support to us since we had got married, adored her grandchildren and now she wouldn't be around to see them growing up. It was hard to accept that she was gone at just 62 years of age. As always Bill was there giving me support and consoling us as a family. As expected, Alison was very upset, she had spent so much of her early years with her grandmother and she adored her. As my mum had been so keen on us joining them for that holiday, I've often wondered whether or not she knew that she was ill and that her time was limited. Sadly, something we will never know.

14

A NEW ADDITION TO THE FAMILY

We welcomed our youngest son Stephen in February 1968, 2 years and 3 months after David was born. He weighed in at 7lbs. exactly. He was born at home with Bill unexpectedly having to act as assistant midwife due to a minor complication. He wasn't expecting that to be on the agenda. He was run ragged that day, I went into labour in the early hours of the morning. He had called the midwife and after dropping Alison off at school he was kept busy carrying out the many instructions she was giving him. Fortunately, a kind neighbour had taken our toddler off his hands for the day. I will never forget the following morning, Bill who had been doing the housework, cooking and washing, had brought me in a cup of tea followed by a bowl with potatoes, a potato peeler and a saucepan so that I could peel the potatoes ready for the dinner. I think he thought he had worked just as hard as me and deserved a break. I protested and said, "I've just had a baby", he said it was occupational therapy as he didn't want me to get depressed. I just looked at him and said "seriously" we both laughed as we suddenly saw the funny side of it.

We were delighted with our new addition to the family and Bill felt he had a special bond with this new baby as he had helped bring him into the world. Thank goodness he was good and a sound sleeper like his older brother. Bill really took good care of us all over the next few days and was a dab hand at changing nappies but then he had to return to work as there was no paternity leave back then and a cold, snowy February was not a good time to be taking holiday leave, so he saved that for the summer months when we could relax and all spend time together as a family. We had already planned for a trip to Ireland, no longer on the overnight ferry but we could now afford to take the midnight flight that was just £10 return at that time.

Our family was now complete and although we had been happy there, our little flat was beginning to get crowded with only two bedrooms and so just over a year later in 1969 we moved to a 3 bedroomed house that had a small front garden with roses around the door and a large rear garden. It was just in the next street so there were no problems with the move. We loved it the moment we turned the key in the front door and from the very first, knew it would be our 'forever home' and the place where we wanted to raise our family. We were happy and had great plans for it and for our future life together.

I can remember during the first week that we had moved in Bill had gone back to work and so I put Stephen in his Silver Cross pram under a tree half-way down the garden hoping he would fall asleep so that I could unpack some of the things that were still in boxes. I was upstairs and looked out of the window to make sure he was alright, to my horror the pram was upside down. I ran down the stairs and out into the garden expecting to find him hurt and crying but all was quiet. As I lifted the pram back up, there he was bouncing up and down like he was on a trampoline. The following year he discovered how to take the brake off when he was left sitting in his pushchair so as a safeguard, we had to strap the wheel to the frame so that he couldn't move it.

This was to be the first year, since we had children that we didn't go away on a holiday as there were things that we needed to get for our new home. However, we did have day trips to the coast, as we now had a car, and took my dad with us as he was on his own.

In his new role as Supervisor covering the north London area, Bill could be called upon out of hours, if an emergency occurred whereby a tree could be considered a danger. It came as no surprise when late one night, during a bad storm, our phone rang. It was the police to say that a tree had been struck by lightning and was lying across the roof of a house, in the Wandsworth area of London. Although it was not an area he covered normally, there was no one else available and so he agreed to go and assess the situation. The London Fire Brigade were at the scene and when he saw the way that the tree was lying, he realised it was in a dangerous position, couldn't be left and needed to be dealt with as soon as possible. There was no option but for him to get up onto the roof of the house to cut it back and make it safe. So harnessed up, armed with chain saw and assisted by the London Fire Brigade he climbed the ladder with no thoughts for his own safety. His first thoughts were for the young family who lived there that had been evacuated for their safety.

The local paper reported the incident and he was mentioned for his bravery. He was commended for his actions by the Police and Fire Brigade for the way he worked throughout the night, on a rooftop in the height of a storm, to save a family home. I would not have expected anything less from him. It was just the way he was, not afraid of hard work and always putting others before himself. The Parks

Department were notified of the incident the following morning and Bill received a letter from the Chief Officer commending him for the work he had carried out which was above and beyond the call of duty, especially as it turned out that it wasn't even one of their trees and was therefore not the responsibility of the L.C.C.

15

A ROAD ACCIDENT

David had not long started school when I had a telephone call from the police one morning to say that Bill had been involved in a road accident and was on his way to hospital by ambulance. I ran across the road to my friend and neighbour to ask her if she would have Stephen while I went to the hospital. She had two girls that were the same ages as the boys so she said not to worry and that if I wasn't back in time, she would also pick David up from school when she collected her daughter and take care of both of them until I got home.

When I arrived at the hospital, I was told he was in X-ray and someone took me to where he was. I was shocked to see him lying there with his shirt covered in blood and blood running down his face from the cut on his forehead. As they were telling me about his injuries, I could feel myself swaying and fell to the floor as I fainted. I ended up in the Casualty Department myself with a nurse giving me tea. In my younger days I used to faint a lot if I was in pain or in shock. When I recovered Bill had been moved to another ward to be further assessed. His forehead had been stitched and he had been cleaned up a bit. He was concussed and had injuries to his leg and damage to his knee. He could only remember leaving home that morning but nothing of the accident. The doctor said he was also suffering from retrograde amnesia and that it was quite common with head injuries and that he might never remember that time before the accident and he never did.

The police said at first that it appeared the tyre had blown on his van and that he had lost control and crashed into a lamp post. There was no other vehicle involved which was surprising as it happened on what was normally a busy stretch of road in the mornings. However, on further investigation of the damage to the van, it appeared that the tyre had more likely blown on impact and that it was possible that Bill had blacked out at the wheel. This could have been due to low blood sugar as he would normally only have a slice of toast in the mornings with a cup of tea before leaving for work; it wasn't enough. The local Council didn't waste any time in sending out a bill for the damage to the lamp post and replacement. The bill was received the following morning. I worried how we were going to pay for the damage caused but one of his workmates who had come to see him, assured me that he was covered by the L.C.C.'s insurance policy and to forward the bill on to them.

When I visited him in hospital the following day, his leg was in plaster and his face looked a complete mess. He had a number of stitches to the cut on his hairline, two black eyes and various bruises and swelling to his face. I was so worried about him; he was always the strong one and now I needed to be strong. A couple of days after he came home, I woke up one night as I could hear him groaning. He was sitting on the edge of the bed holding his head, he was in a considerable amount of pain. I jumped out of bed and rushed round to his side to see what I could do for him. The next thing I knew he was hauling me up onto the bed beside him, once again I had fainted. I was certainly useless in an emergency. Our GP came in to see him the next day and gave him medication for the pain he was in. He was off work for 3 months as being on crutches he was unable to drive.

It's the only time I can ever remember him taking sick leave throughout his working life.

As Bill hobbled around the house on crutches the boys would be behind him copying the way he was walking. They watched a lot of television and could be amusing as they copied the various acts. They loved the Laurel & Hardy films and I can remember one time after having their bath they came downstairs in their pyjamas and entertained us by imitating them. David was always Oliver Hardy and Stephen would be Stan Laurel twiddling his hair and David would be saying "that's another fine mess you've got me into Stanley". One afternoon they were both lying on the floor watching an American series called 'Marcus Welby M.D.' which aired in the early 70s. Marcus Welby was a family practitioner who made house calls. In this particular episode they were watching, the doctor had been called out to a patient who was in labour. As she was in the later stages, he decided that he would take her to the hospital rather than delay the situation by waiting for an ambulance. He made her comfortable in the back of his station wagon and headed for the hospital. On the way, she cried out and he stopped the car and went round to the back to check on her. When he turned around, he had a baby in his arms. I was sitting on the settee and listened to the following conversation between the two boys with amusement. Stephen "where did that come from" David "it was in her tummy of course" Stephen "is it dark in there" David "you should know, you were in there last" Stephen "I couldn't see anything because the lights weren't on". It was so funny listening as they had this serious conversation about where babies came from. David was about six years of age and Stephen four.

My fainting fits became a standing joke and Bill would always say, 'no use calling on you in an emergency'. Many years later and after she was married, we had a call one morning from Alison who had gone into labour with her second child and as her husband had already left for work, she was unable to contact him, no mobile phones back then. She wanted Bill to take her to hospital and for me to look after Paul her 18-month-old toddler. As we drove down to her house Bill said to me "whatever you do please don't faint when we get there, because I can't cope with you, a daughter in labour and a toddler." I did eventually get over my fainting fits much to his relief.

16

WORKING LIFE

From the time we got married and throughout the years of raising a family, Bill always had more than one job and he would do jobbing gardening to earn extra money to make life easier for us whilst also doing any overtime that was available in the early days and before he had become a salaried worker. Whilst working in Holland Park one day, he was contacted by the owner of one of the big houses facing onto the park. It was the home, at that time, of the Canadian Ambassador who needed a part time gardener and so he agreed to do the work that he needed done after finishing his normal day's work, one evening a week.

A few months later he was approached by their neighbour who also wanted a part time gardener and was impressed by his work ethic. He never turned work down and that is when he started working for the Hollywood film producer Charles H. Schneer and his wife who lived in the house next door. They entertained a lot and the garden had to look its very best when they were expecting visitors. Mrs. Schneer would often ring him to say that she was organising a dinner party for the following evening and that she had been to Covent Garden and bought the plants that she wanted in place before her guests arrived. On arrival at the house, he would often find a hundred plants set out for planting. Any plants that were past their best had to be removed and replaced so that everything looked in pristine condition. He never let her down. Fortunately, the Canadian Ambassador had in the meantime returned to Canada some time earlier and so he was able to take on the extra work that she required.

I worried about him and the long hours he was working but he ignored my pleas to cut back. He would go all day with barely a sandwich to sustain him. It was like he was driven by an unknown force to achieve as much as he possibly could in order to be able to provide the best life he could for his family. He never forgot seeing the hard life his mother had had trying to raise a family without sufficient income. He had to make sure that his own family had everything they needed, a secure home and food on the table. Because of the distance, some nights it was 10 o'clock before he arrived home from work and got his evening meal. He was so tired and would fall asleep the minute he sat down.

He saw many Hollywood stars during his time working for the Schneers, among them Telly Savalas, Patrick Wayne and Julie Andrews. He got on well with the family and his work for them was appreciated. I can remember one Easter as I was in the kitchen looking out to the front of the house a Harrods van parked up on the road outside. Not a van you would expect to see making deliveries on a Council Estate. How surprised was I when the driver knocked on our door with a huge box of chocolates; it was an Easter gift, for the family, from the Schneers and the first of many deliveries from Harrods over the years that he worked for them.

As they toured many countries looking for film locations Mrs. Schneer always brought back a small gift for us from their travels. Mr. Schneer was the Producer of many films one of which was the film 'Clash of the Titans' and we were invited to take the boys to the film set to watch the filming of some of the scenes but unfortunately, we were unable to take up the offer as it clashed with our holidays. However, we were given tickets a couple of months later to attend the film premier at the Empire Theatre in Leicester Square where the boys were given souvenir books and mugs. Some of the stars of the film were sitting just a couple of rows in front of us including the actress, Ursula Andress.

When they moved back to the USA Bill continued taking on extra work, but it was mainly private tree work that was better paid and he did it locally at weekends and so during the week, he was able to come home when his day's work was finished and life for us returned, more or less to normal. At one time, due to his high work ethic, he was recommended to act as a consultant, for one of the many London garden squares. These were gated gardens surrounded by big houses. He would meet with the residents of the houses, usually once a month, to give them advice on tending the gardens without having to carry out any of the manual work himself and for this he was paid a good retainer fee every month. He had come a long way from working for the nuns in the convent garden in Belfast.

When the boys were in their teens, he would sometimes take them to work with him when he was doing private work. On returning home at the end of the first day they told me they couldn't believe how hard he worked. They said he did the work of three men. It was an eye opener for them. They learnt from him by example and grew up with the same work ethic.

Bill had now been upgraded to Arboriculture Officer for the North London area that he had covered when he was an Area Supervisor. The area had been extended and split into four with a supervisor and gangs of men in each area. A bonus system was to be set up and some works handed out to contract. He was responsible for setting up the new system in the area that he covered which meant there was a lot more paperwork for him to do and a lot more responsibility. Despite the amount of work and the travelling he had to do, he loved his job and got a lot of satisfaction from what he had achieved over the years. He was very highly thought of by both his superiors and peers, they knew he could always be relied upon. His mum would have been so proud of him, I know I was. He had achieved so much since he left his home in Belfast. He was certainly a father his children could look up to.

17

HOLIDAYS

We had many holidays visiting the family in Ireland while the children were young and I have fond memories of the trips we made to Glencolumbkille in Co. Donegal. These holidays to Ireland enabled Bill to re-establish the bond he had had with his siblings growing up and our children had the opportunity of getting to know their cousins. It brought them all closer together as a family.

I can remember one year that we were on holiday in Donegal with Bill's mum, his sister, her husband and their family. They had six children between the ages of 3 and 11years of age. Alison was 8, David 2-1/2 years and Stephen just a baby. We were staying in a rented cottage that was on a local farmer's land. One afternoon the kids were all playing outside with the elder ones looking after the younger ones. We were chatting inside over a cup of tea and we could hear them all laughing. As I looked up, I suddenly saw David rise up past the window. The other kids were up on the roof and as they had to look after him, they tied a rope under his arms and were hauling him up onto the roof to join them. They got such a telling off, but they were still so full of energy and it wasn't long before the farmer came knocking at the door as they were wrecking one of his haystacks. They were taking it in turn to climb to the top and sliding back down. What a handful they were but they were having the time of their lives.

It was to be our last family holiday there for some time. It was August 1968 when Stephen was six months old and just before the start of the 'Troubles' in Northern Ireland which put a stop to our visits, with the children, for many years to come.

The following year we had a holiday in Devon and as it rained every day of that holiday, it was decided no more holidays in England for us and so started our many trips, while the children were growing up, to Spain and the islands of Majorca and Ibiza. That first holiday to Spain was a package holiday on the Costa Brava. Unbelievably, the cost was £12 per adult for 10 days, full board in a 2-star hotel but that was in 1972 and was a lot of money back then and Bill worked hard to pay for it. I can remember we had a storm during that holiday and all the electrics went out, no lift working and no lights but the staff still managed to serve up our evening meal just a few minutes late with the dining room and public areas of the hotel lit by candlelight.

The second of those holidays was to Majorca and that year Bill's mum was to spend a month with us, two weeks of which were spent on the Spanish island. She loved it, her first and I believe her only holiday abroad. Bill continually felt that it was his duty, to make up for the hard life that she had had and was pleased that he could take her on what was to be a special holiday for her. She thoroughly enjoyed it and one of her daughters had loaned her a two-piece swimsuit and she was made up with it and couldn't wait to get onto the beach and into the sea. David was 8 years old at the time and when he first saw her in it, he took one look at her and said, "Granny you look gorgeous". She was so chuffed at his words. As she couldn't swim the kids had given her their rubber ring. She got it around her waist and paddled out into the sea with no problems until she tried to get it off but she was stuck fast into it. It didn't help that none of us could stop laughing as we tried to get her out of it. We eventually managed it and it was something none of us ever forgot and we would often chuckle when we recalled that memory.

We were booked to go to a nightclub one night and as maxi dresses were in, Bill bought her a long dress in the market, a babysitter had been organised for the kids and that evening we stepped out in all our finery, had a lovely meal in the nightclub and when the dancing started she told us that she would be ok if we wanted to dance and not to worry about her. As we danced, we kept an eye on her but suddenly noticed that the table was empty and we thought maybe she had gone to the ladies but as we continued dancing, I happened to look over Bill's shoulder and there she was dancing with a Spanish guy who Bill thought was holding her far too close and as the dance finished, he quickly ushered her back to the table. She had such a good time and enjoyed the holiday so much. Our holidays were amazing and Bill spent every moment he could playing and having fun with the kids in the sunshine. This was the happy family life he had worked for and he had succeeded in achieving it for his children. They would jump on his back in the sea, share pedalo rides and bury him up to his neck in the sand. It was such a happy time for us as a family.

18

OUR FAMILY LIFE TOGETHER

The kids were still young with Stephen just a toddler when we surprised them with a puppy for Christmas. We had bought a pedigree rough collie. They loved watching the many Lassie films that were around and now they had their very own replica. They named him Rinty and they loved him. He was very easily trained and I can remember that summer as I watched the boys playing in the garden from the window, I saw Stephen toddling off towards the shallow pond in the middle of the garden. It had very little water in it and was covered by a strong piece of wired fencing and so was quite safe. Rinty had been watching him and suddenly jumped up, rushed over to him, took his wrist gently in his mouth and pulled him away from any danger. We knew he would never let them come to any harm.

Rinty was closely followed by two other pets. Bill got them a black and white rabbit that they named Bugsy and a tortoise called Tommy. Pets that he had never known as a child and just something, that for him, helped make us a proper family. When we weren't looking the boys would often smuggle Bugsy into the house to play with them. Like most kids the novelty of looking after him and cleaning out his hutch soon wore off and it was left to me and so I was happy when he escaped from his hutch and disappeared one day. They were heartbroken but I was secretly jumping for joy, one less job for me. My joy didn't last for long however, as one afternoon when they were playing in their bedroom, I heard them shouting out and jumping up and down with excitement, Bugsy had returned and was in the garden, he obviously knew where he was better off. I made sure that they had to take their turn at cleaning out the hutch if they wanted to keep him. No problem caring for Tommy, he had a wired pen at the bottom of the garden and needed very little looking after. It was just a case of feeding him and making sure he had water. He would disappear to hibernate at the start of every winter and return to the garden when the weather got warmer in the Spring. He was always welcomed back with happy smiles.

The only time Rinty was allowed upstairs was if there was a storm during the night, he was very nervous and would howl. I would go down and get him and he would curl up on the floor on my side of the bed and settle down. He would quickly be followed into the bedroom by all three kids as they jumped into the bed between us and dived under the covers until the storm was over. Bill would be pushed out of bed but would stand at the window watching the flashes of lightning that always fascinated him.

As the kids got older, they weren't so good at getting out of bed in the morning and ready for school. We would be calling them from the bottom of the stairs to no avail. Rinty would look up the stairs and then at Bill as if to say, 'leave it to me'. When he got the ok to go, he would race up the stairs and go to each bed in turn and pull the covers off them. That didn't go down well during the winter months when it was cold and we had no central heating.

I remember Bill telling me one day that when he was young, he never had a role model. There was no-one to advise him and guide him in the right direction as he grew up and so he taught his children the values that my dad, his father-in-law who he looked up to, had taught his children. He was Bill's role model and he learnt from him what a good husband and father should be, putting your family before everything and making sure they had a roof over their heads and food on the table. If only his own father had of had the same values, life might have been very different for him growing up but then he might never have come to London for work and our paths might never have crossed. I can only thank God they did.

He could be fiery and had an Irish temper, I think it must have been a family trait as it seemed to run in his family. Several of them were fiery and would often have falling outs but would eventually reconcile. They were fiercely loyal and would always stand up for each other. Whenever there were family get togethers there were often rows between one or other of them especially if they had been drinking and one of them would storm off but they would be over as quickly as they started. Our kids always knew how far they could push their father, his eyes told them when they had pushed him too far and they knew it was time to back off.

I've never been one to argue and so whenever he ranted and raved, I would ignore him and would carry on with whatever I was doing and he would soon get over his outburst when he had got whatever was bothering him off his chest. There was one occasion however, when he was in a temper and ranting and raving, I got so mad with him that I picked up the first thing that came to hand to throw at him. It was a tin of talcum powder and as it went sailing through the air, the top flew off and there was talcum powder everywhere.

We just looked at each other and fell about laughing as tempers cooled.

Whenever he was ranting and raving and saw he was not getting any reaction from me, he would get up, go into the kitchen and put the kettle on. He would then poke his head round the door and say to me, "I'm making a cup of tea would you like one?" that was his way of saying sorry. The twinkle would be back in his eye, I would get a wink and he would smile at me. He never really said sorry after an argument and it made me think of a quote from the film 'Love Story' (loving you is never having to say I'm sorry).

I remember one morning especially when cross words passed between us. I was getting the kids ready for school and doing breakfast and it was bedlam in the kitchen as the kids were bickering and Bill was sounding off at them. Although he kissed me as he went off to work, I was feeling frustrated and tearful as I stood at the kitchen sink, a feeling I am sure many mums have experienced at one time or another. Kids can really push you to the edge at times. As I watched him get into his van. David came up behind me and said "don't worry mummy when he is an old man, I will kick his walking stick out from under him". I had to smile; the things kids say. I mentioned it to Bill that evening after the kids were in bed and although we thought it funny, we both agreed we shouldn't argue in front of them as they were young and impressionable. We made a pact that we would get up an hour earlier each morning and school bags would be got ready the evening before so that it wasn't such a rush in the mornings, we could then have time to sit down and have breakfast together. I don't know how long that lasted but I am sure it wasn't long. The problem was we were all night birds and not at our best in the mornings. Even when there were cross words between us, he never left the house without kissing me goodbye and there would always be a hug and a kiss when he returned in the evening. Cross words that had passed between us that morning, usually meant nothing and were soon forgotten.

19

THE FATHER

From the age of 10 years both boys played for their school football teams and were also signed up with local clubs playing in their individual age groups at weekends. They would play for the school during the week and two different clubs on Saturdays and Sundays. Bill and I always supported them and went to all their games right up until they both left school. As they were playing in different age groups it meant we went to two games every Saturday and two games every Sunday. Sunday lunch for us was very often a Wimpy Takeaway that was eaten in the car as we drove between matches. The Sunday club that David had just started playing for was going on a football tour of Holland. There were four teams going of different age groups but as he was in the youngest group of under-12s Bill felt he was too young to go alone and so he decided to travel with the Club to be there for him. A few weeks before they were due to leave the Manager came round to see me as he also needed a couple of mothers to go for the younger boys and he asked if I could go too. Stephen was 9 years old at the time and so I told him I couldn't leave him but he offered a free place for him too and would give him the opportunity of playing in a couple of the games. That Easter we travelled to the town of Valkenburg in Holland which was to be our base and watched both boys as they took part in the various games. It was a great experience for them and a couple of years later they both did another football tour to Denmark. We enjoyed supporting them during the football years but were not sorry when they finished. It was good to get our weekends back.

We both agreed that the toughest years of our marriage were raising a family. Kids can push you to the limit and ours were no different to any others, especially during those teenage years. Out of the three of them Alison was probably the most difficult. Maybe it was because she was the eldest and handling a teenager was new to us. It didn't help that she was strong willed either. I just remember that when I was in my teens, and I would say it was the same for many of us in the era that I had grown up in; the boundaries were instilled into us and we didn't question them. Also, over the years times had changed and children were beginning to feel their feet and being allowed a lot more freedom than we had. Sometimes it was hard for us to accept the changes. We didn't want to be too controlling and spoiling their fun but we could see the dangers that they never could and our main aim was to protect them and keep them safe. They were our responsibility and we didn't want them to come to any harm or let them down. I don't expect they ever saw it like that though and at times they probably thought we were the worst parents in the world and far too controlling.

I remember one time Alison was sulking in her bedroom as she wasn't allowed out because of some misdemeanour and she wasn't happy because it was the night she would normally go to the local youth club. Bill had heard a noise outside and opened the front door. The noise came from above and as he looked up, he saw our defiant daughter climbing out of her bedroom window ready to sneak out of the house. He stood quietly watching her and as she jumped down from the roof of the porch, she turned around with a big smile on her face thinking she had got away with it, only to come face to face with her father. The smile soon disappeared, one look at him told her she had definitely gone too far this time and was in trouble. She had pushed the boundaries. Not something she ever tried again. I don't know how she planned to get back in and that was probably something she hadn't even thought of. However, it appeared it wasn't the first time she had done this and would unlock the back door before she went out so she could get back in again. I learned this many years later.

Alison wasn't bad but could be stubborn and had that fiery Irish temper like her father and that didn't help as they would clash at times especially when she was in her teens. On his way to work Bill would drop her off at school but as she came down the stairs, he would take one look at her and tell her to go back up and wash the muck off her face and to put her skirt on properly. She was 15 years of age and thought she was grown up and like most teenage girls at that time they would go off to school, if they could get away with it, with makeup on and the waistband of their school skirts doubled over to show their knees – teenage hormones. She would stomp back upstairs mumbling away and slamming every door she went through. In her last year at school, she played truant a couple of times and no way was he putting up with that. He remembered only too well what had happened to him through skipping school, although he was four years younger at the time it had meant 3 years in a Boys Home for him. Her reason for missing school was not because she was being bullied, she just didn't want to be there and it meant she could meet up with a boyfriend who was suspended from school at the time for wearing an earing. A craze that was only just starting.

She was never allowed out late and her time for being in was 10.00pm. If she was 10 minutes late, Bill would be ready to sound off and I would remind him that when we were going out together, I was often late home and a lot later than 10 minutes. He would say quite seriously "that was different, you were with me." If she wanted to stay overnight at a friend's house after a party the answer was always 'no' but she would be allowed to stay until 11.00pm and he would be waiting outside ready to bring her home. Maybe it was because she was a girl that he was extra protective of her. However, as hard as she thought we were at the time, many years later and after she was married with children of her own, she thanked us for how we had brought her up. She hadn't realised how hard it was to raise a family with the right values.

Bill was much more lenient with David and Stephen with regard to the time that they came in. Maybe that was because there was a gap of 6 years between them and Alison and the fact that they were boys. Times had also changed a lot since her teenage years or perhaps it was because she had worn us down. They still had boundaries though and they knew just how far they could push them and quite often they did. He was a strict but fair father and always stood by them even if they got into scrapes and there were a few of those over the years. We didn't expect them to be perfect but we did our best to guide them in the right direction and to teach them right from wrong. We gave them all unconditional love and taught them respect. Bill told them to achieve their dreams they had to work hard and put the time in and he was a good example of that. That was his philosophy in life that you only get out what you put in. He taught them well because all three of them are hard workers and have always treated us with respect and in turn they have brought up their own children to have the same values that were instilled into them when they were younger.

Money was still tight as they grew up even though we both worked full time but we enjoyed a better lifestyle and Bill did extra hours to give them the best life possible with nice holidays every year but most of all the stability that he never had in his young life. Boy were we glad though when those teenage years came to an end. I don't envy anyone bringing up teenagers especially in today's world.

20

THE SON-IN-LAW

My dad was on his own and poorly especially in the last year of his life and Bill would call in to see him on his way home from work. I didn't drive and the boys were still at school and so it was easier for him to check up on him. He would get him something to eat and make them both a cup of tea. What he needed most at that stage was company and someone to chat to and they had always got on so well together from that very first time that I had taken him home to meet my parents back in 1956. As he deteriorated, we called the doctor in who didn't give us much comfort, not our normal family doctor but a locum. She said he was an old man and what did we expect. As he began to deteriorate further Bill would go out earlier in the morning so that he could go in, get him washed and dressed and give him some breakfast before going on to work. We had arranged 'Meals on Wheels' that would deliver lunch for him but when he called in during the evening, he would find it had been left on the doorstep as he wasn't opening the door and so we cancelled that service.

We would go down together at the weekend and I would clean the house, take what needed washing home and bring the clean laundry back the following week. As we sat chatting to him one Saturday morning over a cup of tea, we became aware that he was getting a little confused. One minute he would be chatting away to us and then suddenly he would start talking about his working life when he was a much younger man. We would go along with whatever he was talking about until he came back into the original conversation. I asked him how he was feeling, and he said that he was ok except for his head, he felt like he was two different people. He then said to me 'your mother was in the bedroom this morning", I said "really" he said "yes, she did a little twirl and as she turned around, she left all her clothes on the floor." My mother had died 15 years earlier. I left Bill talking to him and went upstairs to change his bed and clean the bathroom. When I went into his room there was indeed a pile of clothes on the floor but they were his clothes.

When we had arrived at the house earlier, I had stopped to speak to one of the neighbours who was at her gate. She asked how my dad was and I told her that he wasn't great, it was then that she told me that the house lights were on all night and the curtains were drawn during the day. I thought it was strange but didn't really take too much notice of it. It was 1981 and you didn't hear about dementia then or we certainly hadn't. I used to ring him every day and would spend time chatting to him. He always went out each day to get the paper and to collect his pension from the post office once a week. When I asked him during one of these calls if he had been out to collect his pension, he told me whenever he went round to the shops, which were just a five-minute walk away, he said they were never open and that there was just a little light on at the back of the shop. He also said it doesn't get light anymore during the day and that it was always dark. I then remembered what his neighbour had said. Without realising it at the time, this was my first dealings with a dementia patient and at that time I knew nothing about the disease. I wish I had of known and been able to do more for him.

From what we pieced together it seemed he was staying in bed all day and that is why the curtains were drawn and getting up during the night hence the reason for the lights to be on. I think what had happened was that he always used to go up to bed every day to have an afternoon nap but as he was not feeling well, he stayed in bed sleeping longer and longer and so when he woke and got up, it was the middle of the night and his body clock was all out of sync. He started locking all the doors as well. He wasn't eating and appeared to be having trouble swallowing and was losing a lot of weight. As he deteriorated further Bill decided to bring a single bed downstairs for him and called the Doctor again. It was the same Doctor that had called in two weeks earlier. When she examined him, she said, "how long has he been like this?" to which the answer was "since the last time when you saw him and said he was just an old man." She used the phone immediately to ring the hospital and to organise an ambulance for him. She told them that he had pneumonia and was drowning in his own fluid. It was early evening when Bill rang to tell me he was to be admitted to hospital and that he would wait for the ambulance to arrive and then he would come home to fetch me and take me back to the hospital to see him.

When we arrived at the hospital, a nurse came out and told us that he had unfortunately died in the ambulance on his way to the hospital. We were shocked that he had gone so quickly and Bill said if he had of known he was going to pass as quickly as that then he would have asked them to leave him to die in his own home. His death certificate put down the cause of death as heart failure with secondary cause as tuberculosis and so his coffin had to be sealed and we were unable to see him to say our goodbyes.

Most of his family had had tuberculosis when they were young and two of his sisters had died at a young age with it. He was discharged from the Royal Airforce, during the war, on medical grounds as he had been diagnosed with the disease at that time. He returned to work within a few weeks of being discharged, he was a self-employed fence erector and if he didn't work then he didn't get paid and he had a family to keep. When he had a hospital check-up six months later, they were amazed that he was cured. This was put down to him working in the open air. We were told at the time of his death that TB can lie dormant but can flare up again when health deteriorates.

In that final year when he was so poorly Bill would care for him during the week by going in on his way to work and calling in on his way home, getting him something to eat and getting him into bed before he left. He was more like a son to him than a son-in-law, they had always had a close relationship. He had always looked up to him and he had been a role model to him throughout our married life. When he died it hit him every bit as hard as it did me. Nothing prepares you for the death of a much-loved parent. We got through our grief together by supporting each other. I will never forget all that he did for my father in his final years. He was always so caring; I could never ever thank him enough.

21

THE HUSBAND

Bill wasn't just a good father; he was also a good husband. It wasn't always easy for us as money was tight especially during those first few years when we lived in Morden but we usually managed a night out on our wedding anniversary once a year and were thankful for that. My mum would baby sit for us and would have Alison overnight so that we could go to the pictures stopping for fish and chips on the way home. No date nights for us back then, the only dates we got were in a box at Christmas. It was the same for most young couples and there weren't nice restaurants like there are today where you could go out for a meal and people didn't have that sort of money to spend and so we looked forward to that night out that we had at the pictures. Once we moved to Tadworth we were too far away for my mum to babysit for us and any spare money we had was spent on things we needed for the home. While the kids were growing up we never had time on our own but were more than happy to spend evenings, once the kids were in bed, watching television or listening to music snuggled up together on the settee. This was the same for most couples in the late 50s and early 60s.

On the 13th March 1974, our 15th wedding anniversary, Bill arranged for Alison, who was now old enough to look after the boys, to stay in so that he could take me out for the evening. Flowers were delivered for me during the day and a table had been booked at the Gatwick Manor Steak House. We were so looking forward to having this quality time on our own. It was like going out on a first date. As we got into the car, he put a tape into the cassette player and as we drove off Bob Manning's voice came through the speaker singing The Nearness of You, 'his song' that became 'our song.' It was followed by all the songs that had been so special to us over the years. He had stayed up late, after I had gone to bed over the previous week, putting the tape together from our record collection. He had put so much thought into the evening and he had made it so special. He always did have a romantic streak and did his best to make every occasion special for me. Throughout our marriage there were many occasions when he arranged surprises for me.

It was Christmas 1983 when I got the best and biggest surprise ever from him. He handed me an envelope and couldn't wait for me to open my Christmas card. Inside the card was a confirmation from Thomas Cook, the travel agents, of a holiday booking for a 'cruise and stay' holiday for two, departing 15th March 1984, just 2 days after our silver wedding anniversary. We were to sail from Tilbury on Fred Olsen's ship M.V. Black Watch, with visits ashore in Madeira, Lanzarote and Gran Canaria before alighting in Tenerife and staying at the Hotel Aguilas in Puerta de la Cruz which was in the north of the island for a further 7 days. The boys were in their teens, David was just 17 years old and was working as an apprentice paint sprayer but Stephen was still at school. No need to worry Bill said as he had arranged for his brother, who was a merchant seaman and a chef, to take his leave at the same time so that he could stay at our house to look after them as they were still not old enough or responsible enough to be left in the house alone despite what they may have thought.

It was the custom, at that time, that while a ship is at sea you dressed for dinner which meant dinner suits and evening dresses. Not something we were used to. Apparently, unknown to me, Bill had been saving for a long time so that we could have the best time ever. He had planned it to be a belated honeymoon, one that we had waited 25 years for and never expected to have. He apologised and was sorry that it had been a long time coming. No expense was spared and he got so much satisfaction from taking me out and spoiling me, buying evening dresses and two new suits for himself, one of them being a dinner jacket for those formal nights at sea. For once he had spent money on himself as well. He made sure we had everything we needed for the trip and we counted the days to our departure. We had waited a long time to have these two weeks together that we should have had at the start of our marriage. It was, however, well worth waiting for.

It was an amazing experience and at the time the trip of a lifetime for us. I couldn't have asked for more. We had got talking to the comedian Harry Worth who was also travelling on the cruise with his wife. He lived in Kingswood so not too far from us and he would often join us for breakfast in the mornings. He had done the trip many times and was able to tell us a lot about our ports of call. He also worked with the entertainments staff and did a cabaret act.

We met a lovely couple from Redditch who were also on the cruise to celebrate their silver wedding. We had a lot in common with them and like me, Tom was a keen photographer and we both had our Olympus OM10 cameras with us. We spent a lot of time with them and usually had our evening meal together. If it was someone's birthday it was customary for the entertainments crew to come into the restaurant singing the appropriate song for the occasion. Were we surprised when one evening they came in singing 'Congratulations' and stopped at our table. We were presented with a cake baked by the chef and a bottle of champagne, compliments of the captain. That evening when the dancing started, the band played the 'Anniversary Waltz' and we were asked to start off the dancing before being joined by the other passengers. We were so happy. It was such a special time for us.

We had been at sea a couple of days when we arrived in Madeira. We had a trip booked in the afternoon to go to the Botanic Gardens and to do the famous toboggan run down the twisting, sloping streets. We decided that we would go ashore on our own in the morning to wander around the streets of Funchal. After walking just a few steps, I didn't feel right and felt lightheaded, it was as if the pavement was coming up to hit me. I couldn't be ill, so much money had been spent on this trip and we had waited so long for it. I grabbed Bill's arm and just prayed I wouldn't collapse at his feet but he suddenly said that he felt the same way. Surely, we couldn't both be ill. We found a seat and sat down for a while and one of the crew members from the ship stopped and spoke to us as he was about to pass by. It turned out that because we had been at sea for several days, we still had our sea legs which helps you acclimatise to the roll of the ship. Fortunately, after a while our legs got used to being back on firm ground again and so the panic was over.

We had sailed through the Bay of Biscay the day before and were expecting, if we were going to be seasick, then that is where it was going to be. The area was well known for rough seas. However, we were fine although messages were coming over the tannoy speakers calling for the nurse or doctor to go to cabins where people were suffering, there were obviously many who weren't fine. We had great fun with Tom and Dot that evening trying to dance with the ship rocking and rolling. As we took one step forward, we then went six steps back as the ship rolled with the waves. At the end of dancing each night the band had a jam session and we would stay on for that extra hour as the four of us jived to the more upbeat music of rock and roll as we tried to recapture our youth. We were always the last to leave. We were lucky enough for our cabin to be on the boat deck and had a porthole but Tom and Dot were a couple of decks below in an inside cabin, so they found it quite claustrophobic.

There was such a lot of entertainment on board the ship and we were spoilt for choice as to what to do. We tried our luck on the gaming tables and had coffee after dinner in one of the lounges listening to the pianist. We had race nights and would bet on the horses that we could see racing on the video screens. Such an amazing time and when we arrived in Tenerife, we were sad to say goodbye to the new friends we had made who were staying on the ship for the return journey. It had been fun but hectic, so we decided to spend the next 7 days in Tenerife relaxing and having that special alone time together that we had waited for, for so long. As we ate our meal in a restaurant on our last night, Bill bought me a spray of freesias from a passing flower seller. I still have that spray, that I dried when we got home, it is held in a photo album of our trip. Bill had really pulled out all the stops for this holiday of a lifetime. Unbeknown to me he had been planning and saving for it for a long time. It had somehow brought us closer together, the stressful years of raising our family were beginning to pass and we could start to look forward to what was to become 'our time'. At last, he was beginning to feel that all the hard work had paid off and that he was finally achieving all that he had wanted out of life. We were both so happy to have got to this stage of our lives and to still have that closeness between us that had always been there right from the day that we first met.

When we arrived back at Gatwick at the end of our holiday, we were expecting to get a taxi home but as we came through 'Arrivals', Gerry, our three kids, some friends and their kids were all waiting to greet us. Our friend Margaret was holding up a large poster which said,

'Welcome Home'
Rita & Bill
Happy Silver Wedding Anniversary.

It was all back to our house where Gerry, had laid on a spread to welcome us home after a long journey, the celebrations were obviously not over. Something to be said for having a brother-in-law who was a chef. What a welcome home with everyone waiting to hear about our trip. It is one of my happiest memories as I now look back on our life together.

When each of the boys reached 17 years of age, they applied for their provisional driving licence and we paid for them to have driving lessons. They both passed the test first time and Bill helped them to get their first cars. Now we had finished paying for their lessons it was decided that I would also learn to drive. I didn't have the confidence that they had when they had started lessons and I dreaded each week when the driving school car would pull up outside. However,

I persevered and when the instructor thought I was ready I applied for my test. I failed the first time but as it was on a small point I was encouraged to apply for another test and continued to have lessons while I was waiting for a new date.

The following Sunday Bill asked me if I fancied going out for a drive, something we often did on a Sunday afternoon. We had been driving for a while when he parked up and said he wanted to show me something. He started to walk across the road towards a car showroom where he pointed to a car on the forecourt and asked me what I thought of it. It was a silver coloured, Mazda 323 that had a blue stripe along the side. I was a little puzzled as to what we were doing there but just said, that I thought it was a nice little car. He looked at me with that twinkle in his eye and smiled and said, "it's yours, I'm picking it up for you tomorrow." I was speechless, I didn't ever expect to have a car of my own. I didn't know what to say, after all I hadn't even passed my test yet. He said he would take me out in it so I could get in some more practice and build up my confidence. He got as much pleasure out of giving me surprises and buying things for me as I got from receiving them. He couldn't do enough for me and was always showing me how much he cared in one way or another.

We both worked for the same company and so we would drive into work together each morning, in the Mazda, with me driving on 'L' plates. I was so nervous being completely in control of the car and without my instructor beside me in a dual controlled vehicle. The day came for my second test and to my surprise I passed it and could now apply for my full licence. I know that when I got back home, I should have got straight into my car immediately and at least driven around the block on my own but I was absolutely terrified at the thought of being in the car alone. Bill was so pleased to hear that I had passed and when I told him how I felt he said not to worry I would soon get used to it and once I had done a few short trips on my own I would be fine. I'm ashamed to say I never did get behind the wheel of a car again. I would panic just at the thought of it. I was so frightened that I would have an accident. He never once put me down though or pressured me into driving and I felt so guilty that he had spent all that money on a car for me so that I could be independent but never once did he throw it back in my face. He just put the car into our garage in the hope that one day I would get my confidence back and start driving. He eventually took it over himself when his own car started giving him trouble. He was just so good to me; how could I ever repay him for his generosity.

When we had that silver wedding anniversary cruise, I was 45 and Bill was coming up 49. From then on right into our 70s they were the best years for us as a couple, that was our time together, just the two of us. We certainly didn't regret any of those earlier years of bringing up a family, we loved our kids to bits and wouldn't have been without them but money was tight back then and I don't mind admitting that at times it was a struggle and hard work but thankful that I can look at them today and say, 'we did a good job of raising them', they have turned out to be responsible, hard-working adults and they have brought their children up with the same values that they were raised with. We had achieved what we set out to do.

That cruise was just the first of many special holidays, once our kids had flown the nest and for many years Bill organised surprise trips to Paris to coincide with our anniversary. I remember on the first of those trips we had dinner in a little Bistro beside the River Seine. There were only a dozen tables and just a few other couples besides us. It was a very intimate setting and the food and wine were good. The waiters were very attentive and when the bill was paid, knowing we were celebrating an anniversary, one of the waiters gave us a bottle of wine to take away with us. We planned to drink it in our room once we got back to the hotel. Before we went back though we walked onto one of the bridges over the River Seine that was close by and as we stood watching the boats on the river, it started to snow. I felt an arm come around me as he pulled me close to keep me warm. Where would I be without this man in my life. He was just so special. This was a side of the man that only I knew fully and not the man that his children or other family members saw. These were the feelings and love that were shared just between the two of us. We had been through a lot together.

On another night he booked dinner and a show at the famous Moulin Rouge nightclub. Although looking back on that time, I think that night out was more for his benefit than mine seeing how the scantily dressed, topless dancers cavorted around the stage. I was thrilled though to watch the Ballet Montmartre chorus girls dancing the Can-Can. A dance I had always loved since first seeing it performed by a troupe of chorus girls when I appeared in pantomime as a 12-year-old.

We walked all over Paris, visited the Eiffel Tower and all the tourist sites. We went to the Bois de Boulogne and the Bois de Vincennes known as the lungs of Paris. One year we took the metro out to the newly opened Euro Disney. Bill loved the shops and the Paris fashions and I always came home with an addition to my wardrobe.

We did another cruise three years after the first one and again with the Fred Olsen line, this time on the M.V. Black Prince. It was 1987 and a fly/cruise; we flew to Izmir in Turkey where we picked up the ship. We had already started chatting to a Scottish couple on the plane or at least Bill had. When the air hostess came round with the drinks trolley Bill ordered me a drink and two miniature whiskeys for himself. When Alastair, the Scottish guy across the aisle, saw what he had ordered he gave Bill the 'thumbs up' and ordered the same for himself.

Once we had boarded the ship, we made our way to our cabin which again was on the boat deck but this time we had a window rather than a porthole giving us a better view. It was a more spacious cabin than we had before and more luxurious, with a cocktail cabinet and a couple of comfortable chairs as the double bed folded into the wall. We got settled and changed from our travel clothes and went up on deck to watch as the ship left the port. We had dinner and a couple of drinks that evening and had an early night ready for our first port of call the next morning which was to be Marmaris in Turkey. As we anchored out at sea, small boats came out to greet us, full of young people playing loud music and dancing on the deck. We also visited Bodrum, Kusadasi, Ephesus and Olu Deniz whilst on that part of the Aegean coast.

We visited so many ports of call, Dubrovnik, the Bay of Kotor, the Greek islands of Santorini, Corfu, Crete and Rhodes. I can remember when we went ashore in Santorini, Alastair had planned to buy Lyndsey, his wife, a present for a special occasion. She wanted a ruby and diamond ring and he had admired the setting of a ring that I had worn the night before to match my red cocktail dress. When they returned to the ship, we were shown the new ring, it was beautiful and he thought it was a bargain at only £3,000. I didn't have the heart to tell him that my ring that he had admired so much was only costume jewellery and cost me £9.99 from the House of Fraser. I forgot to mention that Alastair had his own business and obviously was not short of a bob or two as besides their home in Glasgow they had a cottage on one of the small Scottish islands and owned a yacht. Their cabin on board ship was not a cabin but a State Room. Nevertheless, we got on well with them, they were very down to earth and didn't put on any airs and graces but obviously he didn't know a lot about jewellery, or did he notice that my ring was worthless but wanted to spare my feelings? Whatever he thought we were to stay in touch with them for many years. Neither Bill nor I had any problems mixing with people that were a lot better off than we were.

One morning, at dawn, we anchored close to the entrance of the Corinth Canal as we waited for the pilot boat that was to guide us through the canal to the Greek port of Piraeus. The canal was so narrow you could almost touch the sides as it sailed through. It was quite an experience. When we docked Alastair negotiated the fare for a taxi to take us to Olympia where the first Olympic games were held, we also visited the Acropolis and Athens. We were surrounded by so much ancient history, places we could only have imagined visiting in our younger years.

One of the highlights of the cruise was visiting Venice, the city of romance. We had spent the day seeing the sites, crossing the famous Rialto Bridge, St. Mark's Square, the Doge's Palace, St. Mark's Basilica and not forgetting the romantic ride on a gondola through the many canals. The day passed all too quickly and it was time for us to return to the ship. The most memorable memory of that trip was our departure from Venice; we were on a high after spending the day seeing the sights of this beautiful and unique city. It had been a magical day and one I will never forget. The ship's band was up on deck as we set sail, we were at the rails watching as the tugs guided the ship out of the port and the band played the Rod Stewart song 'Sailing'. We sailed down past St. Mark's Square as the sun was setting behind us. What an amazing sight and another memory that is imprinted on my mind as we stood there with our arms around each other. We didn't want that moment to end. Venice is such a unique place that we were lucky enough to be able to return to a couple of times in later years and a place where everyone, if the opportunity arises, should visit.

The M.V. Black Prince had a mainly Filipino crew and again after the evening dancing and entertainment there was a jam session that the four of us would stay on for. The band were often joined by crew members who were off duty. There was a young girl of about 18 years of age who was a stewardess when on day duty but would come down to sing with the band when she finished work and was gathering quite an audience. She was certainly wasted as a stewardess as she had the voice of a young Shirley Bassey.

After dinner we would often have a drink in the piano bar. The piano was a white baby grand that had bar stools around the edge of it where you could sit and listen to the pianist. The pianist asked did we have any requests and I asked him to play 'As Time Goes By.' Whenever he saw us walk into the bar after that he would start to play the tune I had requested. Just another memory for us to hold onto.

We were beginning to enjoy the high life and the freedom that we now had without the worry of young children to care for. We would always be there for them if they needed help but now it was time for them to stand on their own two feet. When we got home, we couldn't wait to plan our next trip and Bill would often come home from work with a handful of holiday brochures for us to look through.

We enjoyed having this time together and we made the most of every minute. We weren't ones to lie around a pool all day in the sun and whatever country we visited it was always our aim to explore the surrounding area. From one of our visits to Cyprus, we did a weekend cruise to Egypt travelling alongside the Suez Canal and into Cairo. As our coach crossed the River Nile, we were fascinated to see the feluccas cruising down the Nile with passengers from many countries, as they took a slow meander through ancient history as they would have done in the time of the Pharaohs. We visited the Sphynx and the Pyramids of Giza and recalled the biblical stories from our schooldays. At that time, it was still possible to go inside the main pyramid, we had to bend very low but once we had got through the entrance and were able to stand up straight, we were amazed at how big the interior was. It was fascinating but I found it a bit creepy. I believe it's no longer possible for tourists to enter.

On another weekend trip from a visit to Cyprus, we visited the holy cities of Bethlehem and Jerusalem. In Bethlehem we entered the Church of the Nativity to see the spot where

Christ was born. In Jerusalem we walked the Via Dolorosa (Way of Sorrows) that winds through the old city stopping at the Stations of the Cross as we passed each one. It was the route to Calgary along which Christ carried the Cross on his way to crucifixion. We also visited the 'wailing wall' a place where mainly people of the Jewish faith go to pray although visitors of other faiths are also allowed. Security was very strict there and the armed guards were quite daunting. Bags were searched before going into the area and no photographs were allowed to be taken. The trip was quite an experience and something we were glad we were able to do.

We visited Tel Aviv located on Israel's Mediterranean coast and a kibbutz before returning to the ship and another week in Cyprus.

We had visited most of Europe and so we decided to venture further afield to the Dominican Republic in the Caribbean. Rather than hotel rooms the complex had several buildings spread across the site and each building had four apartments, all with balconies. There was a casino on site and two restaurants. The tour courier told us that there were a few first-class seats available for the return journey at a small extra charge. Bill was right on that and so our return journey to Gatwick was first class on a jumbo jet. There was no joining the check-in queue because as first-class passengers we had our own check-in desk with a 3ft square of red carpet for us to stand on. We were first to board the plane and first off when we arrived back in Gatwick. Our seats were like small armchairs and the service was amazing and there were several goodies on offer. It was just another little extra that Bill had treated us to. We were certainly enjoying this time of our life.

The following year took us to Puerto del Carmen on the Yucatan Peninsula of Mexico, one of our favourite holiday destinations. Just off the coast was the Island of Cozumel which was well known for its colourful sea life. We flew from Gatwick to Houston where we had a six-hour stopover. Rather than stay in transit which meant spending our time in a lounge until the second flight. We chose to collect our luggage and then check it back in straight away for the flight to Cancun so that we had six hours exploring the area and duty-free shops. When we arrived in Cancun, we were met by a limo that was to take us to the Continental Plaza Hotel in Puerto del Carmen. Of all the places we had visited this was one of our favourites. In Puerto del Carmen we had the best of both worlds. We had a modern hotel right on the most beautiful sandy beach with the turquoise waters of the Caribbean sparkling in the sunshine and just a few minutes' walk to the ferry for Cozumel and right on the edge of a Mexican village where we were lucky enough to witness a Mayan wedding taking place. We enjoyed these holidays so much and loved the time spent seeing the local attractions. When we first got married, the thought of visiting these places would have been beyond our wildest dreams. Back then working-class people never even did day trips to France. There just wasn't the money.

Bill would often take me to The Bridge House Motel that sat at the top of Reigate Hill where they held dinner dances. We would sometimes go as a group and other times just the two of us. It was my 50th birthday and Bill had booked a table, it wasn't just for the two of us though as he had arranged yet another surprise for me. On our arrival we were met by our children, their partners and a couple of friends who were all there to help celebrate my birthday. We loved our nights out there whether on our own or with friends. The music was good and we could enjoy the dancing after we finished our meal. Bill loved the Stevie Wonder song 'You are the Sunshine of my Life' that was popular at the time and he would sing it to me as we danced to the music. Those words would be written on the birthday and Christmas cards that he gave me.

When pubs started serving food and operating as restaurants, we used to go out on a regular basis to enjoy a nice meal. Unfortunately, as going out for meals became more popular, bigger groups would gather to hold birthday celebrations and we found it got so noisy that one evening we couldn't even hear each other speak across the table and so we decided to leave and have our after-dinner coffee at home. As it also meant Bill couldn't drink as he was driving, we decided to call it a day on our meal nights out.

We had enjoyed those special meals though and so I decided that rather than give them up I would recreate the atmosphere at home with our favourite music playing in the background. I got out the cookery books and on Saturday nights I would put together a three-course meal and make the evening special as we dined at home by candlelight. We would have a nice bottle of wine and would follow the meal with a liqueur. We would chat away just as we used to when going out for a meal and very often, we would still be sitting at the table until gone 11.00pm. We never ran out of things to say to each other as we were always happy in our own company and never felt the need to be part of a crowd. While I made coffee Bill would put some CDs on which of course always included 'The Nearness of You' and as I put the coffee down on the coffee table, he would take me in his arms and hold me close as we danced to the music that we loved. It was a great way of fanning the flames and keeping the romance alive in our marriage, after all who doesn't like a bit of romance. How lucky was I to be married to this romantic, handsome Irishman?

In 1986, the G.L.C. (Greater London Council) which had replaced the L.C.C. some years earlier, was disbanded by Margaret Thatcher and her Government and so after almost 40 years' service, Bill was made redundant. We already had a holiday booked to Tenerife for July but as he was out of work for the first time since coming to London in 1955, he booked us an extra holiday. We left Euston by coach and travelled down to Dover across to France and through Belgium, stopping in Luxemburg for a coffee break and arriving in the lakeside town of Lucerne the following morning in time for breakfast beside the lake. We were mesmerised by the beautiful scenery as we travelled through Switzerland. The sky was blue, the sun was shining and we were bowled over by the beauty of the area.

We travelled along the San Gotthard Pass where the snow was beginning to melt on the mountainsides, creating narrow waterfalls and on towards Italy and Lake Lugano where we stopped for lunch. It was early April and coming up to Easter. Our journey took us to Milan and on towards Florence where we arrived on Good Friday in time for dinner and an overnight stay. Our room had the tiniest bathroom I have ever seen. You had to walk through the shower to get to the toilet in fact it would have been easy enough to have your shower whilst sitting on the toilet. We visited one of the many restaurants that night for our evening meal before retiring early.

After breakfast we did a tour of Florence visiting the imposing Duomo Cathedral, the famous statue of David and the Ponte Vecchio Bridge well known for its goldsmiths and high-class jewellery shops. Bill bought me a musical jewellery box from one of these shops and it still sits on my dressing table and plays 'Three Coins in the Fountain" when the lid is lifted. There is so much history in Italy and the architecture is amazing. After a stop for refreshments, it was time to depart from Florence and head for the eternal city of Rome which was to be the highlight of the tour and the main reason for doing the trip.

After dinner in the hotel on that first evening, the group moved to one of the lounges drinking and chatting before heading off to bed. We were to spend three nights in Rome and so were able to have plenty of free time to explore. As it was Easter, most of the group chose to head for the Vatican and St. Peter's Square the following morning. We were joined by a Welsh lady from the group as we had breakfast and she asked if she could go along with us that morning as she was unable to wake her husband as he had had too much to drink the night before. I said, "won't he wonder where you are when he wakes up" to which she replied, "no, I wrote him a note and pinned it to his pyjamas".

That morning in St. Peter's Square was quite an emotional experience and for Bill, being a cradle Catholic, it had always been an ambition to visit Rome and the Vatican and to be there when Pope John Paul celebrated Mass on Easter Sunday to the thousands of tourists that had made that journey, for the same reason, was really special for him. It was certainly the icing on the cake. I must say I could feel the emotion myself; it was all around us. There were many disabled and sick people in the square that morning as they waited for the Pope to give his Blessing.

We spent the following day visiting the Villa d'Este in Tivoli just outside of Rome. Such beautiful gardens with spectacular fountains that danced in time to the music. It is where I walked under the fountain of youth hoping it would work its magic on me. Some of the scenes from the film 'Three Coins in the Fountain' were set there so when watching the DVD of the film, I am transported back in time as I recall the memories of our visit. On the return part of the trip, we had a coffee stop in the City of Assisi before travelling on to Venice, our second visit to the city. Three gondolas were booked for the group and we had a singer in the gondola we were in who sang romantic songs, 'O Sole Mio' and 'Anema e Core' as we travelled along the canals. It was very romantic; Bill had his arm around me and it was one of those occasions you never forget. As we glided under the bridges people waved from the top and took photographs of us. It was like being in a film. It was a lovely holiday and we enjoyed our trip through the many countries of Europe. It was on this trip that I fell in love with Italy and it is always on top of my list of places to visit. I have covered most of the country but still have a few places on my bucket list that I am desperate to visit in the south, Ravello, Sorrento, the Amalfi Coast and the Isle of Capri. Places that we had planned to visit one day but unfortunately, we ran out of time due to Bill's ongoing health issues. Hopefully, in Bill's memory, I still have time to fit them in but I feel that time is no longer on my side but fingers crossed.

That summer we were booked on a holiday to Tenerife, this time to the south of island. It was at the time when 'Time

Share' apartments were becoming popular. We went to one of the presentations and were shown around Phase 1 of the Beverly Hills Club in Los Cristianos. It was lovely and they were beginning to sell apartments 'off plan' for Phase 2 which was in the process of being built and due to be completed at the end of that year. Bill was really taken by what we saw and wanted to visit the Sales Office to see the plans of the interior of the apartments and which were available. I was not too sure about going ahead as 'Time Share' at the time had had some bad press and also, I didn't want our holidays to be in the same place every year. I had got used to travelling to different places but Bill was very keen and said that he wanted to buy two weeks in a studio apartment so that we could enjoy some winter sun in November of every year. He had received his redundancy money and could afford to go ahead but assured me that we would still have our summer holidays as usual. When we visited the following year, we were delighted as it was all that we had been promised. We spent the next 20 years having that winter break in the sun and over the years made many friends that I am still in touch with today.

As well as our holidays to Tenerife in November, we would spend our summer holidays, in the later years, visiting the Italian lake areas of Garda, Maggiore and Como. From these areas we took trips into the Dolomites, the Italian Alps, Venice and Verona where we saw our first opera together 'Aida' in the amphitheatre there. What an experience that was. Each lake was so different and each had its own beauty. The scenery was breath-taking.

One of our early holidays was a two-week trip to Sicily. At the time it was new to the British tourist market and it seemed to be mainly Italians from the mainland that spent their holidays there. Back then there wasn't the foreign food restaurants that we have now, so I had never tasted pasta before. I soon discovered that if you didn't like pasta then you didn't eat in Sicily. Even deserts seemed to be pasta based. Very little English was spoken so we got by with the help of a phrase book and basically sign language. No mobile phones with a Google translate App. It was quite an experience for us and a lovely country to visit. We did a coach trip that took us up to a village in the mountains. It was real Godfather country and I was expecting Marlon Brando to come into view at any moment. I am sure it is a lot more touristy now than it was when we visited but somehow, I think too many tourists would spoil the special feeling that the place had.

22

PAY BACK TIME

Bill had done so much for me throughout our life together and I wondered how I could repay him. It was coming up to our Ruby wedding anniversary, 40 years of happily married life together and I wondered what I could do to make it as special for him the way he had made so many anniversaries special for me. I remembered what he had given up for me when we got married and although at the time, he said he was happy to do so I came to realise over the years that it had in fact been a big thing for him to get married outside his faith. So, I decided to see if it was possible to have our marriage blessed in the Catholic Church. The priest was lovely and more than happy to perform a Blessing Ceremony that his Irish family could be a part of. He wanted to meet Bill immediately, he was excited that he was to perform a Blessing for us. I explained that Bill in fact didn't know anything about my plans at that stage as I wanted to tell him on Valentine's Day (ever the romantic) and so he agreed to wait until I had sprung the surprise.

On Valentine's Day I cooked a special meal, got out the best china and cutlery, put on a nice dress and had our favourite music playing in the background throughout the meal. As we were having coffee and a liqueur afterwards, I gave him a card that I had made especially for him giving details of the time and place for our marriage to be Blessed in our local Catholic church. He was quite emotional after he had read it and I knew I had made the right call. I told him that his family were coming from Ireland to be at the Blessing as they had been unable to be there for our wedding.

Unfortunately, his mother had already passed but I knew she would have appreciated what I was doing. He was really chuffed and couldn't quite believe it and I could tell it meant a lot to him. We both looked forward to the date 13th March 1999. Of course, this meant we had to start going to Mass on a regular basis although over the years we did normally go at Easter and Christmas and so we went on the following Saturday morning so that Bill could meet the priest after the service. At the end of the Mass Fr. Gerald said he had an announcement to make. He had some very exciting news to tell the congregation. He said, "sitting behind 'so and so' and in front of 'so and so' on the left-hand side of the church there is a lovely couple who want their marriage Blessed on the occasion of their 40th wedding anniversary." He was very excited about it as he said it was like the prodigal son coming home as Bill had strayed off course. Well, we were ready to dive under the pew in front as all eyes were upon us. He then went on to invite all the parishioners to the service.

We had a lovely day and the parishioners had arranged for refreshments in the church hall afterwards. We followed this with lunch at the Derby Arms a local pub on the Downs and a party at home in the evening. After this we felt obliged to go to Mass each weekend. 3 years later I converted and was received into the Catholic Church, in a candlelit ceremony, during the Easter vigil service in 2002 at the Franciscan Friary in Chilworth with Bill's brother and sister attending.

23

AFTER REDUNDANCY

When he was made redundant after almost 40 years of working for the Greater London Council, he was paid three months money in lieu of notice and so during that period he could not take on work. He used the opportunity to do some landscaping in the garden. He laid a fairly substantial patio incorporating a pond and waterfall. Considering he had not done that type of work before he did a good job and that patio is still in good condition some 30 years later and is still well maintained. However, due to the amount of upkeep, the pond was replaced, by our son Steve, with a decked area in later years.

His final employment was the position as Estates Manager for the Pharmaceutical Company I had been working for in Epsom for 8 years. He was responsible for the grounds which covered 26 acres. No longer did he have that long, tiring journey to and from London each day and so his days working locally were much shorter and we were able to travel backwards and forwards to work together.

It wasn't until the hurricane of 1987 that I realised just how dangerous Bill's job as an arboriculturist had been. The telephone rang early on the morning of Friday 16th October telling him that trees had been blown down during the overnight hurricane and were blocking the entrance to the main site where we both worked. He was surprised to get the call as although the noise of the wind had kept me awake most of the night, he had slept through it.

He was employed by the Company as an Estate's Manager but it was for horticultural rather than the tree work that he had done throughout most of his working life. However, they knew he had the necessary experience and qualifications required for the job. He still had his equipment from the many years he had worked as a tree surgeon and so was able to load what was needed into the boot of his car. I often walked to work and would go through the footpath into the back entrance. I couldn't believe the devastation in front of me, many trees were damaged and some completely lifted out of the ground. I heard the familiar noise of a chainsaw and watched as Bill, on the roof of one of the buildings, cut back a tree that was lying across it. My heart was in my mouth, I saw how competent he was but realised how dangerous it could also be but he was back doing the job he loved.

Five years later the company merged with an American Pharmaceutical Company and we were both made redundant. I took the opportunity to retire from work but Bill was offered work with the contractors. However, he was advised that financially it would be more beneficial for him to accept redundancy and then apply for a job with the contractors who were to take over the maintenance of the grounds. He worked for them for another year before finally retiring himself.

I was so proud of him for all he had achieved in his working life since first arriving in London. He had worked so hard and was thought of so highly by his peers and those that had employed him. It was now his time to sit back, relax and enjoy his retirement years. Bill sit back and relax? That was never going to happen and so he still did some jobbing gardening locally for people he knew until he was 70. I was also asked to do some accounts work for a local building company and so I did a couple of days a week until Bill finally hung up his gardening gloves and even then, I continued helping the building company but worked from home in my own time so I had no set hours and we could spend most days together. I guess we both found it hard to give up, we were always workers and used to a working life. At least now it was by choice and not because we needed the money.

There was hardly a day that went by when he didn't say he loved me in some form or other, he didn't have to say it in words, I could see it in his eyes, by the way he treated me and by the way he looked at me, his smile and that wicked wink just confirmed it. His love was unconditional and I've never ever regretted one moment of our life together. It might seem that I am looking back on our life together through rose-coloured glasses but that isn't the case. I am well aware that it wasn't all moonlight and roses but then marriage never is and how boring it would be if it was. There has to be give and take on both sides. It would be very boring without a row or two and I would say that most mornings cross words would pass between us especially during those years we were raising a young family. Those words never meant anything but were just a way of getting rid of pent-up emotions. We had our ups and downs but we never stopped speaking or went to bed on a row and we never stopped loving each other. After all the best part of a row is the making up.

Throughout our life together the family were always our first priority. It doesn't matter how old your children are, in your eyes they will always be your children, you never really see them as adults and you still feel that need to protect them and support them. In later years we were to see two of them go through broken relationships, a separation and divorce and we were there to listen to their problems and dry the tears that fell. Our family always came first and that is what being a family is; to always be there for each other. It was a sad time for us too as we had always hoped that our children would find the same happiness that we had had throughout our life together but life has changed in so many ways and not always for the better. It was a different world to the one that we had grown up in.

When Alison, as a single parent, was struggling to raise two children under four years of age, it brought back memories to Bill of his early years as he recalled seeing the struggles his own mother had had raising a young family on her own with very little help. Although times were not as hard in the 70s as they had been for his mother all those years ago when the country was at war, he wasn't going to see his daughter going through the same thing his mother had gone through and so he would call in every Thursday on his way home from work with a couple of bags of shopping to see her through the week. Amongst that shopping there was always a treat for our two young grandsons and so they would look forward to his visits because they always knew there would be a treat for them. We would go down at weekends to make sure she was managing ok and to take the boys out to buy new clothes when needed. Bill would also tend to her little garden to make it a nice, safe area for the children to play in.

Broken relationships are always hard especially when children are involved. It was particularly hard for our son too as it meant being parted from his children as they were still of school age and living with their mother. He was devastated and it took him a very long time to get over it but eventually he was able to move on, find happiness again and make a new life for himself.

It was hard for us to accept how things had turned out for two of our children. We had just assumed that they would have long, stable relationships like we had had. Our youngest son has managed to stay the course and has been married for more than 25 years and in a 10-year relationship with his wife prior to that. However, it was a different time and life had changed so much from our years together. Couples that married back in the 1950s like we had, tended to stay together, whereas that's no longer the case. Life is much more materialistic now as well.

We were blessed with 7 grandchildren and 6 great grandchildren so far and adored every one of them. When any of their birthdays came around, while they were small, Bill and I would take them out for the day. A favourite trip for all of them was the Bluebell Railway where we would take them to ride on one of the old steam trains. There were trips to the Aquarium at Brighton, Birdworld and many other places of interest. On the way back we always had to stop at one of the Little Chef restaurants so that they could get a burger and an ice cream. Sunday mornings I would take three of them to the local leisure centre so they could learn to swim. They are all swimmers now except for me but I enjoyed that special time with them. At Christmas I would take them to McDonalds for a treat and then onto the Playhouse to see whatever pantomime was showing. Such special memories of times spent with our grandchildren as they were growing up. We were so lucky.

Christmas time, when the grandchildren were young Bill would dress up as a very authentic looking Father Christmas.

One year he was knocking on our front door and two of our young grandsons rushed to see who it was. They stopped dead in their tracks as they saw his silhouette through the glass door and said, "its Father Christmas". We told them to open the door and let him in. As they opened the door and Bill was about to step over the threshold, Stevie who was the youngest, said to him, "take your boots off" which was obviously something he was used to hearing before going into his own home. Bill would come in with sacks of presents and plenty of ho, ho, ho's. When he had finished handing them out, he would say he was very thirsty and would like a glass of whiskey to warm him up before his journey home. As he was handed the whiskey their eyes would almost pop out of their heads as he would lift up his beard to take a drink. As he got up to leave, he would tease them and say that he thought their nanny was a bit of alright and he would pick me up in his arms and say he was going to take me back to his home in Lapland as he headed towards the door. They would shriek and cry out and say, 'please don't take our nanny away'. One year as we waved him off at the front door, a small boy came running round the corner, he was visiting his grandparents who were neighbours of ours. As he saw Bill, he stopped dead in his tracks, turned around to his dad and said, "look who's here dad". It was a special moment for that little boy as Bill bent down and took his hand and shared a few words with him. He enjoyed these times just as much as our grandchildren did. We had such fun with them all at Christmas when they were small. Memories that will stay with them and me for always. They were such special times so full of love and those happy memories the older grandchildren still talk of today.

24

CHRISTMAS IN BELFAST

One year we were going to Ireland for a surprise 60th birthday party for Bill's sister and as her birthday was on the 23rd December it meant staying over for Christmas. Bill decided to take his Santa outfit to surprise all the kids on Christmas day. We were sitting listening to Christmas carols on Christmas Eve when the security lights came on outside the house. The blinds were lifted to see what had set them off. It was just before midnight and snow had started to fall and continued throughout the night. It was magical, it was such a lovely scene and reminded me of the film 'White Christmas' when the snow they had been waiting for suddenly started to fall.

We had a big family lunch on Christmas Day with other members of the family joining us soon afterwards. All the kids were beginning to get restless as they knew there were still more presents to come and so Bill went off to get into his outfit. When he was ready, he went out of the back entrance and made his way to the front of the house with a sack full of presents triggering the security lights. The blinds were up so as the lights came on, he was visible to all the children through the window. They all went quiet and just stood watching him not sure what they should do, he banged on the window to tell them to open the door, it was still snowing and cold and icy outside. The door was opened and he came in full of the usual ho, ho, ho's. There were more sacks full of presents inside. He was given a chair to sit on and told the children to sit on the floor in front of him. He sat chatting to them for a while and then started handing out the presents. As each child received presents from him, they could be heard saying 'thank you Father Christmas'. He was given a glass of whiskey before he left to resume his journey. The children all ran to the front door to wave him goodbye; the front garden was on a slope and it was bitter cold and he wanted the children to go back in so he could nip round to the back of the house to get in and change his clothes but our David and nephew Paul had other ideas and kept encouraging the children to stand and wave and the pair of them were shouting out 'we'll see you later at 'The Stagecoach' (a local bar) for a drink. The language he was mouthing at them was not the usual language Santa uses. It was good fun and I am sure all those kids who are now adults still remember what was, a special Christmas for them that year. We all partied late into the evening and I think it was one of the best Christmases we ever had in Ireland. The whole thing had been recorded and when we watched the playback when we got home, we noticed that when he was handing out the presents the children were all saying, 'thank you Father Christmas' but when it came to our young granddaughter Dannii, she quite clearly said 'thank you granddad'. Nobody picked up on this at the time and then she just carried on as if he really was Father Christmas. Christmas was always a special time for us as a family and I have very fond memories from those years.

Our grandchildren are all grown up now with some of them married or in relationships and with children of their own and so now we have great grandchildren. Our family is expanding and from just the two of us three generations have been created. It is always a pleasure when any of them come to visit. We especially love to see the babies and the toddlers as they remind us of when we were starting out and raising our own family.

When we both retired our time was ours to do as we wished. We enjoyed our holidays together while we still could and while health issues permitted. When the weather was fine, we spent a lot of time in the garden. It was Bill's pride and joy and from the time we first moved into the house in 1969 it had been nurtured and gradually landscaped as and when we had the money to spare for buying plants and shrubs. He especially loved dahlias, fuchsias, rhododendrons and azaleas and so throughout the summer months the garden was always full of colour right through to the autumn. He planted roses to climb up the trellises and tree saplings that have reached maturity and in early March the magnolia tree is covered in blossom and looks beautiful. A Japanese maple and a liquid amber tree are spectacular when the leaves turn to red and gold in the autumn and we have all year colour from the various shrubs that he had planted. The work isn't quite so hard now and it is just a case of cutting the grass and pruning back roses and other shrubs and of course there is always the weeding. I helped where I could but he liked to do it himself and so I tended to just plant up pots in the spring.

We spent many an hour relaxing on the loungers, drinking tea or coffee and many an evening when the weather was fine, we would have our meal on the patio and chat together as we shared a bottle of wine. Spending time together like this always came easy for us, we had the same likes and dislikes. We were quite happy in our own company and did not need to be surrounded by others, we had such a lot in common and were more than happy just being together. Those moments that we shared were precious, we were good together. How I miss those times Looking back on our life I don't think I would change a thing, not even those difficult early years. Surviving that time just made us stronger as a couple and when we got that first home of our own, we really appreciated what we had and were able to put those early years behind us. It was to be a new beginning. You need to experience the tough times to be able to appreciate the good times and that was certainly true in our case.

True love needs no words; I saw it every day, in his eyes, in his smile and felt it in his touch. Our love had survived the many years that we had been together because of the respect and love that we had for each other. Could I ever replace him? Most definitely not. I was a one-man woman and he was my first love; there was never anyone before nor could there be anyone after.

He Was My First, My Last, My Everything

PART TWO

25

A DECLINE IN HEALTH
LEADING TO DEMENTIA

Diabetes: Apart from being diagnosed with a duodenal ulcer in the first year of our marriage, when he was 24 years of age, Bill was fairly healthy until his mid-forties. It was 1981 and my father had passed away; a secondary cause on his death certificate had been recorded as tuberculosis and as close family contacts we both had to have a medical check. We visited our GP and answered his questions with regard to our general health and how we were feeling. I was ok but Bill mentioned that he felt listless a lot of the time and was always thirsty. A urine test showed his sugar levels were high and he was referred to the Diabetic Clinic. On his referral he was diagnosed with Type 2 Diabetes and it was decided that, as he was overweight, it could hopefully be controlled by weight loss and so we went to see the dietician to discuss how we could adjust his diet and what foods he needed to avoid.

Bill was someone who liked his food and had a hearty appetite and so it was not going to be easy for him having to cut back on the foods that he loved. However, he adapted to the restricted diet well at first, lost the required weight and as his sugar levels came back to normal, he started to feel a lot better. It was, however, to be the start of regular six-monthly hospital visits so that they could monitor his condition. In order to help him keep control he was provided with a diabetic testing kit to check his blood sugar levels each morning by pricking the tip of his finger and placing the testing strip into a machine to get a reading which he then had to record for his next hospital appointment. Provided the reading was within the range given then he knew he was ok.

Unfortunately, he had a very sweet tooth and so it wasn't always easy for him to keep to the diet, especially after he had reached the required weight and so from time to time, he would have the odd treat. He loved puddings and was partial to a biscuit and a cream cake and basically anything that was sweet. When I say 'a biscuit' that normally meant a handful. He would make a cup of tea and while in the kitchen he would be tempted to dive into the biscuit barrel. It was hard for him to keep to the strict diet and to keep off the sweet foods that he loved so much. He was a grown up and therefore old enough to be responsible for his own health, so I wasn't going to nag him because I felt that it would have had the opposite effect on him. This was something he had to control himself. The dietician had given us a diabetic cookbook and so I was able to balance his diet as best I could by using the recipes recommended. There wasn't a lot of difference between the recipes in the book and what I was already cooking for the family, they just needed to be adapted slightly. It was the sweet stuff that would be the problem and much harder to control. There were also cakes and puddings in the recipe book and so I would make him things like scones and rock cakes which he was more than happy with. I also only bought plain biscuits and I would give him a couple with a cup of tea instead of him helping himself and so he was happy for the time being.

After a couple of months on the restricted diet, with the odd, sweet treat, he maintained the weight that the hospital had recommended for his height. His blood sugar levels were in the right range but to me he looked ill, his face was looking haggard and drawn and his clothes were hanging on him. Family and friends passed comments on how he looked and were worried that there might be something seriously wrong with him. He didn't seem to have the same energy as he had had before and I thought the weight loss was too drastic for his height and frame size. His next hospital appointment was due, so I decided to have a word with the doctor and dietician. They said that maybe he could go nearer to the top of the weight range for his height rather than sticking to the bottom of the range which had been suggested initially but no higher. As his weight increased, he began to look and feel a lot better and his energy levels returned. It was just a case of getting the balance right.

He did eventually have to go on medication as the blood sugars could no longer be controlled by diet alone and many years later in 2003, he was put on Lantus insulin which meant he had to inject; something he was not looking forward to. Fortunately, the insulin prescribed was long-acting and so he only had to inject once in a 24-hour period which he did before going to bed each night and so it didn't cause too many problems or affect his lifestyle.

Heart Attack: In the summer of 2005, we were going on holiday to Ireland. We had an early flight that morning and had booked a taxi to take us to the airport. Bill had chosen to sit in front with the driver giving him more leg room. I noticed that he seemed to be a little agitated and I put it down to tiredness and the early morning flight. Neither of us were good first thing in the morning; we were known night owls. However, we had a taxi driver who appeared to have verbal diarrhoea; he never stopped talking. We basically ignored him as most of his babble didn't require an answer anyway but then he got onto the subject of politics, not a subject for early morning travel and his political views were the exact opposite to Bill's at that time and I knew it would rile him. He was praising the Margaret Thatcher Government, who were in power at that time and saying what a good job they were doing of running the country. It was like a red rag to a bull for Bill who was already agitated. It was the Government that had abolished the G.L.C and as a result he was made redundant from a job that he had loved and had been in for almost 40 years so naturally he was a bit anti. Fortunately, we were just coming into the airport and the ensuing argument came to an end. As we entered the airport and made our way to the check-in desk there was a long queue as the desk wasn't open and so Bill said he was going off to get a newspaper. In the meantime, the queue had started to move and I was beginning to panic in case he wasn't back by the time I got to the front as I couldn't check in without him. He suddenly appeared and thankfully he looked a lot calmer. He said he had had terrible indigestion but had bought some Bisodol tablets and was now feeling much better.

On arrival in Ireland, he seemed to be back to normal at first. The occasion and the reason for our visit was for our Godson's confirmation and Bill was to be his sponsor. I was seated on the other side of the Church during the service but as I looked across at him, I thought he looked flushed and that he didn't look too well. He definitely hadn't been himself for the past couple of days. When I asked him if he was feeling ok, he said yes and not to worry he just felt a bit tired and he put that down to the journey. We were staying with a nephew and his wife and were to travel up to Donegal for a few days to stay in a traditional Irish cottage that they had bought. The weather wasn't great but it was a lovely break for us as we toured the local area; an area we had grown to love from the family holidays we had had there when our children were young.

I was still concerned about Bill and he was obviously worried himself as the night before we were due to return home, he spoke to his nephew who was a paramedic. He asked Bill a few questions and after chatting to him he did a couple of tests to check him out. As a result, he advised him to arrange to see his doctor when he got home as we were due to leave the next day. He had an appointment arranged for the Monday morning, assured me that he was feeling ok and drove himself to the surgery. I was due back at work so told him to ring me after seeing the doctor to let me know how he had got on.

I had only been in the office for half an hour when I got a call from the surgery to say that an ambulance had been called for him and he was on his way to hospital. The receptionist told me not to worry, that it was not a blue light call but the Doctor had wanted him to lie flat. Fortunately, I wasn't too far from the hospital as it was within walking distance. When I arrived, he was already in 'resus' and being attended to and I was asked several questions regarding his general health. I explained how he had been the previous couple of weeks and after receiving the results of the tests that had been carried out, we were told that he had had a heart attack at some time during the previous 10 days. He was admitted and spent the following week in hospital for further tests. Considering what we were told, I suspect that he was having that heart attack when we were on our way to the airport and that explains why he was so agitated in the taxi. What he had thought was bad indigestion was actually a heart attack.

During one of the hospital visits to see him, he told me that he didn't want to drive anymore. I was a little surprised but knowing that he had had a heart attack that he was not aware of, I think it had frightened him and he was worried in case it happened again whilst he was driving and could cause a fatal accident. He was 71 years of age and had already had to give up driving at night due to vision problems associated with his diabetes. I supported him in whatever he chose to do. It wasn't a problem for us as we had good transport links and we could always get a taxi if need be. The amount of traffic on the roads had increased so much over the years that driving was no longer a pleasure anyway, so I think he was quite relieved especially with his eye problems.

Advanced Diabetic Retinopathy: He had advanced diabetic retinopathy and from time to time needed laser treatment to treat the growth of new blood vessels at the back of the eye. The new blood vessels tend to be very weak and often cause bleeding into the eye. Treatment does not help to improve the vision but can help stabilise the changes caused by the diabetes and stop the vision getting worse. However, this had reduced his night vision and he was affected by the oncoming headlights and so he no longer felt safe driving at night. I can remember one day after receiving such treatment he woke up the following morning and called out to me, he sounded in a panic. I went into the bedroom and asked him what was wrong; he said "I can't see anything" I told him to sit still and try to stay calm while I rang the eye hospital where he had had the laser treatment. I explained the situation and they told me to keep him quiet and as still as possible and bring him in for a check up. Within seconds of me finishing the call he said his sight was beginning to come back. I helped him to get washed and dressed and rang for a taxi to take us to the hospital. Fortunately, his vision did return after a matter of a minute or so but for him it was scary and he possibly felt that the vision loss was for a lot longer than it actually was. The probable cause was put down to a leaking blood vessel that had temporarily affected his vision. Thank goodness it wasn't more serious; he had enough problems to contend with.

Vascular Peripheral Disease: The heart attack was followed by several TIAs and on-going vascular problems causing severe leg pain. He had been diagnosed with Vascular Peripheral Disease, causing intermittent claudication due to lack of blood flow to muscles during exercise or in Bill's case during walking causing him severe leg pain that would ease after stopping to rest. He was advised to try to walk through the pain but it was difficult for him. However, over time the condition got worse causing him pain even while resting. It became so painful at night while he was in bed that he got very little sleep and so to avoid disturbing me and keeping me awake at night he moved into the other bedroom and watched TV until exhausted he would fall asleep. Claudication is a symptom of VPD which is a narrowing of the arteries in the limbs that restricts the blood flow. Because he was getting severe pain even when resting, over the next few months he had Angioplasty in both legs. This procedure improves blood flow by widening the artery and so the blood flow into the leg is easier. This helped the situation and for a while he was free from leg pain. However, due to his declining health, he was on statins for high cholesterol, medication for high blood pressure, he was diabetic and a smoker, all problems that affected his condition.

He had been a long-term smoker, from leaving school and starting his first job at the age of 14. It was 1948 and nearly everyone smoked and the long-term damage that it could do was not known of then. Several times he had tried to give up the habit due to his health concerns and as more dangers that smoking could cause, came to light. By this time, he had been smoking for almost 60 years. He tried wearing nicotine patches on his arm but would still yearn for a cigarette and in fact still had one. A nicotine patch is a transdermal patch that releases nicotine into the body through the skin. One morning I walked into the bedroom when he had just put a new patch on his arm and as he was about to put his shirt on, I told him that he still had the previous days patch on his other arm. His answer was that maybe it still had some nicotine left in it and so he left it on. He also tried chewing nicotine gum. It was clear that the nicotine patches were not the answer for him; he was soon back on 20+ cigarettes a day.

After some routine blood tests, it was noted that he was anaemic and so tests were organised to find the cause of possible blood loss. It was arranged for him to have an endoscopy and a colonoscopy. He never complained about having any tests no matter how unpleasant they might have been. He had to return to the hospital to get the results from a doctor and was told that they couldn't find any signs of blood loss and so they were putting him on iron tablets. During the appointment he took a bout of coughing and the doctor asked if he had a cold, he just replied that it was probably a smoker's cough. The doctor said, "not necessarily" and said he would refer him to the Royal Surrey Hospital, Guildford for further investigation. When the appointment came through it meant an overnight stay so that they could do a biopsy early the next morning and he was told the results would be sent back to his doctor. On receiving the results, he was referred to a throat specialist and was told he had pre-cancerous cells in his larynx and that they would keep regular checks on him. Despite being advised to give up cigarettes, he was still smoking; he couldn't seem to accept that it could be causing all the problems he was having. I guess he had been smoking for so long that it was hard for him to stop. I was always with him when he had appointments, so we always faced any problems together and I made sure he stayed on track with his medication and controlling his diabetes.

Cancer of the larynx: It wasn't until a few years later that he finally gave up for the first time when in 2008 he was diagnosed with cancer of the larynx. He was referred to the Royal Marsden Hospital where he had successful radiotherapy treatment. This was to be followed by periodic checks over the next 5 years, at St. George's Hospital in Tooting. Halfway through the check-up period and despite all the warnings, it wasn't long before he was back smoking again. Giving up was so hard for him despite the health scares. Many people would not understand why he could not give up but would you tell a drug addict to stop taking drugs? Like drugs, smoking is an addiction and one that he had been on since he left school at 14. At the end of the 5-year period he was thankfully given the all clear but just when we thought all serious health problems were over his vascular problems got worse and his mobility was causing problems.

Vascular problems resulting in surgery: Through his visits to the Diabetic Clinic, he had annual vascular scans and it was after one of these scans that he was referred to a Vascular Consultant. I was with him as he was told that because of blockages, he needed surgery to put a stent in his stomach and a bypass to his groin. However, the Consultant said that although he was able to carry out the procedure, he could only do so if Bill gave up smoking. He went on to say that if he didn't give up smoking, then his mobility would eventually get worse and without the necessary surgery could result in the need, at some stage, for both his legs to be amputated from the hip. That was like a smack in the mouth for both of us, we had no idea that the vascular problems were so serious; we walked out of the consulting room in shock. Neither of us could speak and the first thing Bill did when we got to the hospital exit was to light up a cigarette. That was the last cigarette he ever smoked. The thought of losing both legs had really shocked him; it was a wake-up call. He was determined never to buy another packet of cigarettes again and he gave me the pack he had that still had a few cigarettes in and asked me to dispose of them. I rang our GP when we got home and explained the situation and she immediately prescribed a course of Champix tablets. Between the shock diagnosis from the Vascular Consultant and the medication prescribed, it did the trick and the smoking stopped.

Three months later in April 2013 he had the necessary surgery at St. Peter's Hospital in Chertsey, which we were told had been a success. We waited anxiously at the hospital until later that evening when he was brought back onto the ward from the recovery room. He was in great form and to our surprise was sitting up in bed and chatting away to us. At last, we thought all his health problems were finally over and we were delighted but how wrong were we when less than 24 hours later it all went wrong. Little did we know that it was to be the start of almost 5 years of decline due to Vascular Dementia.

As we had spent several hours at the hospital waiting for him to be brought back onto the ward and he appeared to be fine, his sister who lived nearby, said she would do the afternoon visit the next day and the plan was for us to go back that evening. During her visit however, he became agitated, was asking for me and wanted to know where I was and so she rang my mobile so he could speak to me. He wanted to know when I was coming to collect him. He had got himself dressed that morning but had been stopped as he tried to leave the ward to go home. I reassured him as he appeared slightly confused and I told him I was on my way and would be there soon. In view of the apparent change in him from the previous evening, we decided that we would go to the hospital earlier than planned and so I went with Steve and Alison who had come home from Spain where she was now living. When we arrived, we found that he had been moved from the room he had been in earlier that day and we had to ask where he was. We were told to take a seat in a waiting area and that somebody would let us know when we could go in to see him.

It was some time before a doctor came to see us. Whilst waiting, we had noticed a lot of activity and toing and froing of nurses and doctors into one of the wards. It was explained to us that Bill was very confused and aggressive, he had pulled out the cannular and wouldn't let anyone near him, so they were going to sedate him. We were asked to wait until he had calmed down before we could go in to see him which was several hours later. The curtains were drawn around his bed and they allowed us to stay with him, even though visiting had finished some time earlier and the other patients had been settled for the night. Whilst we were there a nurse came in to take his blood pressure, but he started to get agitated again and was trying to fight her off; Steve reassured him and told him that we were there with him and that everything was alright. Hearing a familiar voice, he settled down and she was able to do the necessary checks. Later that evening the doctor came back and said they were taking him for a scan as they thought he may have had a brain bleed. As he had calmed down on hearing familiar voices, they asked one of us to go into the x-ray room with him. Steve went in whilst we waited outside. We were in shock; how could he have deteriorated so quickly from our last visit just 24 hours previous. Once he was back on the ward and had settled down to sleep, we left. It was after 11.30pm and we had been at the hospital since 6.00pm.

Dave who had been in Tenerife on holiday but was on his way home had been told before boarding his flight that his Dad had come through the surgery ok and was in good form. By the time his flight had landed the story was so different and he too was shocked when he first saw him. It was such a worrying time for all of us and we kept his family in Ireland up to date with his condition.

Although still somewhat confused he did in fact improve over the next couple of days and so he was moved back to the vascular ward. There were six other men on this ward who were all recovering from vascular surgery. Bill was the only one who had both his legs. The rest of them had all had amputations and the patient in the next bed had had both of his legs amputated. Bill was lucky, he had got off lightly.

The confusion was still a problem and after a few days he was seen by a doctor for the elderly, who asked him the normal questions that are asked when they are checking for signs of dementia. He was able to tell us all about the doctor and the questions he was asked when we visited that evening. He made us smile when he told us how stupid the doctor was, who knew absolutely nothing about history and how he had sent him off with a flea in his ear. He had told him that if he didn't know the dates when WW2 started and finished then he wasn't fit to be a doctor and needed to go back to school and get himself an education. Despite being confused he was able to answer correctly all the normal questions. Just over a week later he was discharged with a letter to his GP suggesting that if the confusion did not clear up within a few weeks then an appointment should be made for him at the memory clinic.

The day came for us to collect him from the hospital. Steve who lives just 5 minutes away from us was to pick me up and we would go to the hospital together. He was so excited that his Dad was coming home and he couldn't wait to see him and to settle him at home in familiar surroundings. The past couple of weeks had been a strain on all of us especially as it was a journey to get to the hospital. We borrowed a wheelchair from the ward to get Bill down to the ground floor where we transferred him into a hospital wheelchair that we could take out to the car park. Steve had left us by the coffee shop while he went back up to the ward to return the wheelchair. While we were waiting for him to return, I said to Bill how sad it was to see the state the other patients in the ward were in. He just looked at me and said, "they should have gone through what I've been through". I was surprised to hear his reply as it was so out of character for him. I explained to him that they had all had legs amputated and that one of them had lost both legs and if he hadn't given up smoking that could have been him. He looked up at me with tears in his eyes and said, "I'm so sorry, I didn't know". He was full of remorse and realised how lucky he had been. The story could have been so different.

On the drive home he sat in the front passenger seat and was noting the different road signs that we were passing; there were signs and directions for Heathrow airport and he picked up on the names of several of the towns and villages that we drove through and although he didn't associate them as places that he knew but instead said "their towns have got the same names as our towns have" which we thought was quite strange as he had appeared to be ok when we left the hospital and not particularly confused. Steve gave me a questioning look as he caught my eye in the rear-view mirror. When we got home, we had to park the car a little way up the road and as we walked back down to the house he said, "that didn't take us long to get home did it and we didn't even fly over the sea." We put this down to the fact that as we left, he saw signs for the airport. He had not been in a local hospital hence the reason for him seeing the names of the various, surrounding local towns and villages that we would not have normally passed through had the surgery been carried out locally. As several of the nursing staff had foreign accents and the orderly who served his meals was Spanish speaking, he thought he had been on holiday and that now we were home, although for the first time he didn't recognise our house as being his home and wanted to know whose house it was. This was often the case whenever we returned after being out, although strangely enough he always knew the correct address where he lived.

Over the following weeks the confusion gradually improved as he recovered from surgery and had settled in at home. Alison had returned to Spain, so the boys and grandchildren all came in to see him on a regular basis and he enjoyed their visits. Having a close family unit made such a difference and I appreciated their help and concern for him. Early one evening when our granddaughter called in to see him after she had finished work, he was sitting in the conservatory and as we were chatting to him, I said I was going to the shop to get some fish and chips. He began to get very agitated and appeared frightened; he didn't want me to go outside of the house as he said it was too dangerous and he was worried that I would come to harm. He kept looking out of the window and asked me to stay with him. I reassured him and told him he wouldn't be alone as Dannii was there with him and said that I would be safe so not to worry and that I wouldn't be long. When I returned just 10 minutes later, she said he had got very upset whilst I was away but as soon as he saw me, he settled down and ate the fish and chips I had bought. I didn't take too much notice of this at the time as it was early days and so he hadn't fully recovered from the surgery. In view of his age and what he had been through, I expected some confusion from time to time.

As he got stronger and his mobility began to improve, there were days when we could get the bus, go into town, wander around the shops and stop for a coffee. He couldn't walk too far though as he would get tired and so I bought a transit wheelchair for him which was lightweight and easy for me to fold up and take onto the bus. He loved it when we stopped for a coffee. We would sit at one of the tables that looked out onto the shopping centre so that he could watch the passers-by. Wherever we went over the years he always enjoyed stopping for a coffee and a scone or even better still a cream cake. He loved people watching and so it kept him occupied and he was more than content just watching the world go by.

Over the next few months apart from short periods of confusion particularly when he was tired, he seemed to be getting back to his old self and enjoyed family visits especially when any of our great grandchildren came, the youngest two were just babies and he would love to bounce them on his knee the way he had so often done when our own children were young.

I noticed over the following weeks that when the light began to change and as dusk descended, he would start to get agitated and a look of fright would appear on his face as he kept looking around him. He would look out of the windows and towards the front door that he could see from his seat in the conservatory. He would often say to me that we needed to get our coats on and to go home before it got too dark. He appeared to be afraid of the dark. When I told him that this was our home, he got angry with me and said I was trying to confuse him. During the day he would be fine apart from getting a bit forgetful from time to time. We would sit and chat together, watch television and listen to music.

Over the course of the following months the periods of confusion didn't go and if anything, they increased especially during the early evening. He had an appointment for a diabetic check up with our GP and I mentioned the problems to her and asked if she could refer him to the Memory Clinic as had been suggested almost a year earlier after the vascular surgery. We had to wait a couple of months for that appointment.

Vascular Dementia – A life changing diagnosis: The doctor at the Memory Clinic spoke to us separately at first and then together. She mentioned to me that when she spoke to Bill, he was very confused and couldn't answer many of her questions which I was a bit surprised about as he hadn't appeared to be that confused before we arrived there. I then realised that a possible reason was that whenever he was seen by a doctor, I was always with him so very often, if he hesitated, I answered the questions he was asked without realising it. When he was on his own, he wasn't able to answer a lot of the questions for himself, so the problem was obviously worse than I had first thought. When he was asked how many children he had, he said there were five children. I told her we only had three but that he was actually one of five children. She said she would arrange for him to have an MRI scan on his brain to see what was going on. We had a second appointment with her, a month later, to get the results of the scan which showed that there was some deterioration to his brain and he was diagnosed with Vascular Dementia with possibly some signs of Alzheimer's. Over the following months there were to be many changes to our lives.

It was obvious that this was a life changing diagnosis for us. I knew absolutely nothing about this disease only that for Vascular Dementia, I had read that there was no cure. Whereas, with some other dementias such as Alzheimer's whilst there is no cure there is medication that can be taken to slow down the progression of the disease. With no cure Bill had been given a death sentence and the situation could only get worse. Where do I go from here? I needed to make a decision as to how best to handle the situation we found ourselves in. It wasn't going to be easy. As far as I was concerned going into a care home when things got worse, was never going to be an option for him. He had spent 3 years in a Boys Home when he was just 11 years old which had had such a big impact on his young life and I was going to make sure that, as long as I was able, he was never going into another home. I felt it was my duty to care for him the way he had cared for me and our children throughout our married life together and apart from that it was what I wanted to do for him. I didn't want us to be apart for one minute and I knew he would have felt the same. I wanted him here with me, I had made a vow the day that we married:-

I, Rita Ann take thee William John
to be my lawful wedded husband,
to have and to hold,
from this day forward,
for better, for worse,
for richer for poorer,
in sickness and in health,
to love and to cherish,
till death us do part.

After almost 60 years of married life, I had no intention of breaking any of those vows that I had made on Friday 13th March 1959. He had been true to the vows that he had made to me, on that day so long ago, throughout our time together.

I Was To Live With Dementia For The Next 5 Years: It can be a lonely life as you watch your loved one slowly drift away from you. Dementia has been described as 'the long goodbye' and that's just what it is like. Whoever described it as such would have experienced living with the disease at first hand and probably for a long time. One minute we were in a close loving relationship and then suddenly things started to change. At first it was just little things that were hard to make sense of. One minute he would be fine and we would be chatting away together and then suddenly, he would start talking about something completely different, something I couldn't relate to, something that had happened possibly years before I even knew him. He would look at me with such a vacant look in his eyes as if I was a stranger and then within the blink of an eye he would carry on with the original conversation. I then remembered that this had happened one day when we were talking to my dad in his final year way back in 1981 but we didn't take too much notice of it at the time as we had no knowledge of dementia and just put it down to the general confusion of an elderly sick man.

During the early stages of dementia, changes are very subtle and may not even be noticed, especially by outsiders. As Bill's problems seemed to start after the vascular surgery, we thought the possible cause for confusion was as a result of having an anaesthetic at an older age. I had read of similar cases where this had happened. However, as he began to recover from the surgery and settle down at home in familiar surroundings, he seemed to improve. His appetite also began to return. Days like this were easy to cope with and we were able to sit down for a chat and watch television together. He could go hours or even days without any problems and then suddenly something would happen when you least expect it and this would be followed with some confusion often when he was beginning to get tired.

Over the following weeks and months, the periods of confusion increased although there would be weeks in between when he would appear to be back to normal. He was in the very early stages of dementia. I was lucky in some respects that I was retired, reasonably fit and healthy and so I was able to make the decision to care for him myself. It is not a decision everyone can make as everyone's circumstances are different and not everyone has the stomach for it or even the strength to see it through. You also need support from other family members where possible. I don't think I could have done it alone. If I was to be able to cope and take care of him myself, which is what I wanted to do, then I needed to do some research into the disease itself. I needed to prepare myself for what lay ahead. I knew I could rely on the family for support and that they would be there for both of us but little did I know back then just how soul destroying it would be. It is a big undertaking but it never entered my head to take any other path than the one I took. He was my world and I wanted to keep him in it for as long as I possibly could and to do all that I could to make life a little easier for him. I wanted to show him how much we all cared, how much we loved him and that we would always be there for him just as he had always been there for us.

It was about this time that I started to lose my hair, I had discovered some bald patches. Although it was only the early days of dealing with his dementia, I was beginning to find the situation stressful as I knew so little about it. I bought some Nourkin tablets that I had seen advertised as stopping hair loss and promoting growth. I also felt I should get checked out by the Doctor and so made an appointment. She told me the Nourkin tablets were safe to take and also prescribed a hair thickening shampoo for me. She put it down to what I was going through at that time and said the problem was stress related. The tablets and shampoo seemed to work and the hair loss did eventually clear up, thank goodness.

Understanding Dementia – online course by the University of Tasmania: I spent hours researching the internet and reading books that others had written about caring for loved ones with dementia and hoped to pick up some tips. Although they helped immensely, every case was different and no two cases were alike but I still didn't feel that it was enough. Then one day I saw an advert, that came up on my Facebook feed, for a 'free' online course that was being run by the University of Tasmania (The Wicking Dementia Research and Education Centre) MOOC (Massive Open Online Courses) called 'Understanding Dementia'. Signing up for this was the best thing I ever did. Not only was it very helpful, but it was also very interesting and gave me something to focus on. I was fascinated on the section of the workings of 'the brain' which at first, I thought would be boring and hard going but it helped me to understand how the brain works and how it becomes infected by this cruel disease.

The course was done over a 12-week period and I was able to do it at my own pace providing it was finished in the given time. I would study after Bill had settled down for the night and so while he slept, I would be on my computer studying and reading up on the various stages of the disease sometimes into the early hours of the morning. I felt so driven to find out what I could about this life changing situation in the hope of making the life he was facing just a little bit easier for him whilst at the same time maintaining his dignity. At the end of each section, I had to complete a test by answering correctly all the questions asked before I could move onto the next section. I learnt so much from this and there was also a link where it was possible to interact with others that were also doing the same course for the same reason that I was. We were able to chat with each other and discuss what problems we were facing and how each of us handled the various situations we found ourselves in. This was invaluable as we were able to pass on tips to each other on what worked for us as every case was different and what worked for one did not necessarily work for another. There were a lot of people in the same position that I was in and they were doing the course for the same reasons. I was surprised that there were some nurses also doing the course but discovered, that back then dementia was not included as part of a nurse's training and maybe they also had loved ones who had succumbed to the disease that they wanted to help. I learnt how others coped with the different situations that they were being faced with and that in turn enabled me to cope. I also no longer felt alone, as there were thousands of people out there who found themselves in the same position that I was in.

I completed the course in 2015 a year after Bill was first diagnosed. I also discovered, much to my surprise, that there are many different types of dementia. It appears that in some cases Parkinson's Disease is also linked with dementia. Although initially the main problem with Parkinson's is with movement, some patients after a few years have problems with thinking, memory and perception. Around a third of people with Parkinson's go on to develop dementia. There also appears to be a link between 'type 2 diabetes' and dementia and in fact in some medical research dementia is being called 'type 3 diabetes'. Although not everyone who has type-2 diabetes will go on to develop dementia. I found this interesting as in Bill's case, he was one of a family of five, four of them had developed 'type 2 diabetes' in their later years and three out of the four of them went on to develop dementia. Bill with vascular dementia, a sister with alzheimers and his brother with lewy body dementia. All different types of dementia, similar in some ways but completely different in other ways but just as devastating.

Preventing Dementia – a second course by the University of Tasmania: The following year I was invited by the University to take part in another course 'Preventing Dementia'. Although dementia cannot really be prevented it is thought that there are steps that can be taken, throughout our lives, to improve the chances of possibly keeping the disease at bay as we get older. A lot of it is focussed on the middle years of life, obviously staying healthy, not smoking and drinking in moderation but also further education was a big advantage and by keeping the brain active it was able to increase its memory capacity. Unfortunately, all too late in Bill's case. He had always been a manual worker and in the middle years of his life he was more into his favourite hobby of gardening than further education. This gave him many happy hours and for him it was relaxing and rewarding. He would be in the garden in the summer months until it got dark. I always knew where he would be, I would see the glow from his cigarette and there he would be sitting on his bench at the bottom of the garden enjoying a smoke. Sometimes I would join him with a coffee and we would sit and chat about our day.

For anyone who is facing life caring for a loved one who has dementia and if they are able, have the time and are computer literate, I would thoroughly recommend doing either or both of the MOOC courses and finding out all they can about the particular disease they are coping with as it will certainly help to make life just a little easier and hopefully help the carer to understand the complexities of the disease.

I was very proud to receive diplomas for each of the courses I had taken. A year later I received a further communication from the University inviting me to continue with the study of dementia by working towards a degree. There was a substantial cost for this course plus it meant making a 5-year commitment. As Bill was now heading towards another stage of the disease his need for my attention was increasing and as I was heading towards 80 it wasn't feasible for me to continue. I had achieved what I had set out to do and that was to gain the knowledge that would help me cope with the situation I was facing at that time. I don't regret, for one moment, taking part in either of the two MOOC courses and would thoroughly recommend them to anyone who finds themselves in the same position as myself, for me they were invaluable. If I had been a lot younger and not committed to being a caregiver I would have considered going further in the study of dementia. The University of Tasmania still run these, 'free on-line' courses together with the Wicking Dementia Research & Education Centre. Information can be found on their Facebook page or on their website.

I remember someone saying to me, on first hearing that Bill had been diagnosed with dementia; "thank goodness its nothing serious, they just forget things". Don't be fooled, whatever type of dementia has been diagnosed, it is so much more than that. It is not just a case of forgetting things but also for the patient the loss of language and memory solving skills. There is no miracle cure and although there is medication for some types of the disease to slow the progression down, it is not an easy fix and does not work in all cases. In 2022 the

World Health Organisation estimated there were 55 million people worldwide living with dementia. Due to a rapidly aging population this is expected to rise to 78 million by 2030. There is a lot of research being done into finding a cure for the disease and some progress is being made but more money needs to be invested into that research.

We had thought, at first, that the onset of Bill's dementia was as a result of the surgery he had had in 2013 and the effects of having an anaesthetic in the later years of his life. Although he wasn't finally confirmed as having vascular dementia until early 2014, his cognitive skills had deteriorated quite rapidly after the surgery. However, over the past couple of years and since I started writing his story, I have recalled a couple of other minor incidents that had occurred where he had said things and done things that were completely out of character for him. I never made any connection that there could be something wrong and just put it down to age and so these minor incidents were soon forgotten but something strange had happened at least two years earlier that, looking back on now, I should have picked up on but as it was a one off and I had no knowledge of dementia at that stage, I had forgotten all about it.

Missed signs: We had travelled to Tenerife on holiday, something we had done every November for more than 20 years. In the later years, Bill usually had assistance at the airport due to his mobility and after getting off the plane he would be taken through arrivals, by wheelchair, to the taxi area. On this particular occasion, in 2012, before getting a taxi to our resort he wanted to have a cigarette and when he had finished it, he decided before continuing our journey, to go back into the airport to use the toilet, so I waited with the luggage, just outside the exit door. More than half an hour later as he had still not returned, I went looking for him. I asked someone to check the toilets for me to see if he was still there but he wasn't. I was beginning to panic as I couldn't see him anywhere and was getting worried. I then saw the girl that had assisted him earlier with the wheelchair when we had first got off the plane and as soon as she saw me, she called out to me to go with her to the Information Desk where Bill was sitting in a wheelchair and two members of staff were caring for him. They told me he seemed confused. What appeared to have happened was that he had turned left instead of right when he came out of the toilet and the fact that the airport was very busy and full of people, he had got confused and had forgotten where he was. It hadn't helped that the exit had been changed to the other end of the airport from our previous visit. Having found him the girl took us both straight to a taxi for our onward journey.

As the taxi left the airport, he was very quiet at first and then he got angry with me and said, "don't you ever leave me like that again." I just agreed as he was acting strangely, I didn't want to get into an argument with him whilst we were in the taxi. Once we were on our way, he started to recognise the areas we were passing through and began to perk up and started chatting as though nothing was wrong. By the time we arrived at our destination he was back to his normal self and looking forward to our holiday; it continued with no other mishaps and the incident was never mentioned again.

Although I thought this was very strange at the time and he didn't seem to know what had happened to him there were no further instances and so as time went by, I forgot all about it. However, I was reminded of the incident a few years later when I was reading a book written by John Suchet, who was caring for his wife who had dementia and exactly the same thing had happened to her as they travelled to their home in France. In her case there were two entrances to the toilet and she had come out of the wrong one and didn't know where she was. Until I had read her story, I had forgotten all about our experience in Tenerife. This was obviously the start of our own dementia story.

Another incident had occurred on one of our holidays to Lake Maggiore in Italy although very different to the first one. We had been having such a good time until one evening, in our hotel room, he suddenly changed and started to accuse me of all sorts of things and we quarrelled because I didn't know what he was talking about and he accused me of lying. That evening we didn't go out. The following morning when I got up, I was still upset about his accusations of the night before and was very quiet and didn't want to speak to him. He asked me what was wrong. When I told him about the quarrel that we had the previous evening he didn't know what I was talking about and thought I was making it up. I said nothing more about it as I didn't want to spoil the rest of our holiday and once again the incident was forgotten. Neither of us ever held a grudge after an argument and we would just move on but there was one strange thing that happened on this particular holiday that we both found unsettling.

We had got talking to an older couple, on our first day, who had asked us had we been to Lake Maggiore before. We replied that it was our first visit and they said it was their daughters favourite place and that she had lived there for a year. I asked if she was with them to which the mother replied "yes, she is in my handbag". We both looked at each other as she then went on to say that their daughter had died and they were there to scatter her ashes and were wanting to find a suitable place. I must say at the time it gave me the creeps but for some reason it really seemed to spook Bill and whenever we were in our room, he said he would get this strange feeling and felt there was a presence there. Although he was fine all the time that we were outside of the hotel, he did his best to avoid the couple as he felt there was a connection to them and how he felt when he was in our room. In our early years together, he would often talk about his growing up in Belfast and of haunted houses and spirits. Something that a lot of Irish people seem to believe in. I'm not sure that I do but maybe he thought the room was haunted although I never ever noticed anything strange about it. I wonder, if the way he reacted was another early sign of dementia like the Tenerife incident?

The couple never did find a suitable place to scatter their daughter's ashes and took her home with them. I guess they just weren't ready to let her go. Looking back on those incidents now, how come I didn't link them together? I guess it was the lack of knowledge about this dreadful disease or maybe I just didn't want to accept the fact that there was something wrong.

For some time, we were still able to have meaningful conversations with each other although there were periods of confusion usually towards the evening when he was getting tired. In the early stages there were often good days when we would sit and chat recalling memories of our life together. We talked a lot about our children growing up, the things they used to get up to and the arrival of our grandchildren. We would sift through the many holiday photographs and recalled the places we had visited over the years. So many happy memories but all too soon, those memories for him began to slowly disappear especially the more recent memories. Although strangely enough a lot of the long-term memories were still there at that time.

He would come downstairs each day and if it was nice and bright, he would sit in the conservatory listening to his music. Other times he would sit on the settee with me and we would watch television together or I would put on a DVD so that he could watch a film. He was always a great movie fan. One of his favourite films was The Quiet Man that had been filmed in Ireland in the village of Cong. As we travelled around the country on one of our holidays visiting Counties Galway and Mayo, we took the time to visit the village which is on the borders of the two counties where the film was set. It is in such a beautiful area of Ireland and I will always have special memories of such visits to look back on. Over the years we travelled all over Ireland and I was impressed by the Irish hospitality. It is one of the nicest countries to visit with spectacular scenery.

We both loved music and had a large collection of vinyl records and CDs spanning the years. I downloaded more than 250 tracks onto an iPod Nano that I had bought him for his birthday. I connected it to an external speaker as he didn't like using headphones and so listening to the music became a big part of his day. I would often hear him singing along to the music, sometimes he would have tears in his eyes and he would look so sad as the music reminded him of a particular moment in his life. Wherever Bill was, then his music went with him. In the good weather when it was warm enough to sit in the garden, in the conservatory, the kitchen or in his bedroom. Whenever he got agitated this was the one thing that would calm him down. The magic of the music was so powerful and was such a big help in caring for him and was something we could both enjoy. We would often sing along together to the music we had loved, he really enjoyed that and we passed many a happy hour in that way. The one thing he never forgot right to the end was the words to the songs that he loved. He would only have to hear the first few notes of the music and he would know immediately what the song was.

Sundowning: Bill was admitted to hospital several times, especially as the disease progressed, this was usually due to UTI's or other infections. These infections usually affected his mobility and he was at greater risk of falls. He was normally discharged within a week but I can remember on one occasion however when I visited, he had been moved to a single ward near to the nurse's station so that they could keep an eye on him. A nurse told me the reason he had been moved was because he was getting restless each evening, usually around the same time and was getting agitated and she asked me if I knew what was causing him to act in that way. I explained to her that it was probably sundowning as he would do the same at home as dusk approached. She had never heard of it because there was no dementia training at that time for nurses. I started to visit earlier so that I was there at the time the sundowning started and I was able to distract him.

Sundowning appears to be a common occurrence of dementia and one that, at first, I found hard to understand.

I would say most patients irrespective of what type of dementia they have will experience this at some stage. When Bill first started having these symptoms which was as he moved towards another stage of the disease, he was sitting in the conservatory, the light was beginning to fade as the sun went down and he started to get very agitated. He was peering out of the door and through the windows. He seemed to be frightened and was asking to go home. He got very upset and angry when I told him that he was home. He told me to stop lying to him and confusing him. In the end I found it easier to agree with him rather than try to correct him. I would do my best to distract him, I would close the blinds and switch the lights on as soon as the light started to dim. It appears that as the sun goes down and dusk falls, shadows are created and the patient misinterprets what they see and becomes confused and afraid.

The one thing that always worked to distract him when he was confused or agitated like this was to make a cup of tea, put his music on and have a singalong with him. This is how I coped with the sundowning and the many other difficult situations I had to face. Whenever we sat in the conservatory, he would often ask me if I would sing to him. I would sing along to the music that was playing in the background and he would join in. When the song finished, he would say to me, "you're in good voice tonight Reet". I was only singing along with the track but the voice he heard over mine was probably that of somebody like Ella Fitzgerald. If only I had a voice like that. Thank goodness he never forgot the love he had for music over the years and many a time it got me out of trouble. It became a lifesaver for me. It helped that we had grown up in the same era so we had the same taste in music.

If he still started talking about going home, then I would say, "as it is getting dark why not stay where we are and then go home in the morning when it is light". I said, "do you not like it here?" and he would reply "yes, I do like it here it's a lovely house but what about the people whose home it is, won't they mind?" I made the mistake of telling him that it was ok for us to be here as it was our house and we had bought it. That really worried him because how could we have possibly had the money to buy our own house. His mind had gone back no doubt to his poor beginnings when money for his family was so hard to come by. I showed him the deeds which showed our names as the joint owners and how much we had paid for it in 1980. He got even more agitated and worried about where the money had come from. I explained that we had been paying rent to the Council but then we got a mortgage and paid the money to the Building Society instead. He couldn't accept my explanation and I quickly had to change tact and said that the people who owned the house had said we could stay for as long as we wanted to. He was happy with that and said it was a nice house and he would like to stay.

I soon realised that I had to be careful what I said to him, he was in a different world now, and one that was nothing like the one he had known before. I couldn't bring him back into the world that we had known together but I had to join him in this new world he found himself in.

It was sad to think that the home we had loved and shared together and where we had raised our family, he no longer remembered. Maybe the house that he remembered was the house that we had moved into when our children were young. We had made many changes over the years as we had modernised it but those memories had been lost and so it was no longer the house that he remembered or maybe the home he was talking about was the one back in Belfast where he had grown up. That is something we will never know.

He had loved the garden that he had nurtured throughout the many years of our life together. Even though he no longer remembered that it was our garden and that he had planted the trees when they were just saplings and the shrubs when they were no more than small plants that had now reached maturity. He enjoyed the days when it was warm enough for him to be able to sit on his bench and look around at his surroundings. I can remember the times, before dementia, when he would walk around the garden and as he came across a lovely flower; he would cup the bloom of the plant gently in his hand and say to me "look how beautiful that is". He loved how a small cutting that he had taken would very soon turn into a beautiful plant that would burst into bloom each year. He loved the scent of the blooms especially from the many roses he had planted around the garden although he would be disappointed when a beautiful rose had no scent to it at all.

A struggle with visitors: He began to find it difficult if we had visitors which would usually be family. It was ok if just one came in to see him but even then, his attention span would be short. If it was more than one and they were all talking to each other he would get confused. Not only could he no longer join in their conversations but he could also no longer distinguish the words when more than one person was speaking. At first, he would sit up and show an interest but within five minutes he would just lean back in his chair, close his eyes as if he was asleep and go into his own little world. It was as if he just switched off and so we tried to limit the number of visitors who came in at any one time. It is hard for anyone who knows nothing of dementia and how it affects the brain to understand this. That is why it is so important to find out as much information as possible before committing to caring for a loved one.

It was about the same time that he no longer knew who his sons were. He knew he had two sons but the sons he remembered were the teenage boys that lived at home and they were David and Stephen which is what they were always called when they were younger and he worried that they no longer came in for their dinner at night. Our sons were no longer teenagers but were grown men with families of their own. He knew the Dave and Steve that came in to see him but at times he saw them as his mates rather than his sons. When this happened it must have been very upsetting for the boys that he no longer knew who they were and I felt for them. When I knew they were coming in I would say to him, as I heard the key turn in the door, "that is our David who has come in to see you" or "that is our Stephen" so that when they poked their head around the door and said, "hello dad" he would reply and say, "hello son".

Alison lived in Spain so we didn't see quite so much of her. When Stephen was small, she used to sing a popular song of the day to him that was called 'Lollipop' and was sung by the Chordettes and so he started to call her Lollipop as he couldn't pronounce her name properly as he was eight years younger than her and that name stuck. Whenever I told Bill that Alison was coming home to see him, he would keep asking me "what time will Lollipop be here. He always seemed to know her and I think that is because she reminded him of the younger version of me. There were times he would say to me "where is Rita" and I would say "I'm Rita" but he would just say "no not you the other one". There was no point in trying to correct him as this would just make him even more confused. I would say, "maybe she is downstairs shall I get her for you" and he would nod. I would walk out of the bedroom onto the landing, turn around and walk right back in again, he would look up at me, smile and say, "there you are, I wondered where you were".

Thank goodness through my research I was able to understand how these situations affected him. I felt for him, this wasn't the same Bill I had spent more than 60 years of my life with but a different Bill than the one I had known but still very much the love of my life and I realised that in times like this I had to be a part of his world. He was unable to join me in mine.

It is difficult to understand what the patient is going through and how someone else's brain is reacting differently to yours in every-day situations. A lot of what he wasn't understanding now I think is similar to how a young child doesn't always understand. It seemed to me that as the disease progressed, the brain seemed to be in reverse mode and every-day things that had been taken for granted had suddenly become new and complex.

Extra care: I was his sole carer for almost 3 years but after being admitted to hospital with a UTI the Occupational Therapist wasn't happy to discharge him without a care package being put in place. She felt that caring for him alone 24/7 was too much for me and thought I needed help. I was quite indignant and said that I was more than capable of caring for him myself. I had managed so far and I didn't want anyone else taking over. However, the boys suggested I give it a try for just a couple of weeks as they were worried it was beginning to take its toll on me as his condition was deteriorating. I agreed to a two-week trial period and an agency carer was organised to come in for 45 minutes each morning to get him up, washed, dressed and settled in his chair ready for breakfast. He was to return for 30 minutes in the evening to get him into pyjamas and settled into his bed for the night. When the two-week period was up, I had to agree that it had been a big help and that whilst the Carer was there, I was able to do other jobs that were beginning to get neglected and so I agreed to having the help that we paid for.

Andrew was Romanian and an excellent Carer and spoke very good English; we couldn't have asked for better. When he first arrived, I introduced him and explained to Bill that he was here to help me care for him as it was beginning to get too much for me and that I needed him to assist me. I told him that I would still be there and looking after him, but that Andrew would get him washed and dressed while I got his breakfast ready. He was happy with my explanation and the fact that I would still be around for him. Andrew was very kind and gentle with Bill and he soon settled into the routine. When he arrived in the mornings he would touch Bill's arm, say good morning to him and ask him how he was and if he remembered him. Bill would say 'yes I think so' but at first, he couldn't always remember his name. Andrew would sometimes say to him, "I'm Andy Pandy," the name of a puppet from a children's tv show and Bill would look up at him and smile.

I usually got him up in the morning and out of bed, made him a cup of tea and would have him sitting in his chair ready for his arrival. Sunday was Andrew's day off and we would have Nicholas, another Carer who was also Romanian and a lovely guy who was very kind and helpful too. These two carers were all a carer should be and an asset to the care system. It also helped that they both had a very good command of the English language and the right approach in dealing with a dementia patient. They had had very good training.

As Andrew washed him in the bathroom in the mornings, Bill sang along with the music he could hear coming from his bedroom. It was a Max Bygraves medley of old songs that Bill enjoyed. One of the tracks was 'Show Me The Way To Go Home' and much to my surprise, one day, I heard Andrew join in and sing along with him. Apparently, a lady that he had cared for previously used to sing the song all the time and so he knew the words. I often heard them singing along together and enjoying themselves until one morning, some time later as he approached another stage of the disease, Bill stopped singing and I heard him say, "you're not allowed to sing that song, that's my song".

As the dementia progressed, the singing stopped and he would be quiet as he was being washed and dressed and in that little world of his own. The music was still very much a part of his day-to-day life though and would help to keep him calm. He forgot many things but one thing he never forgot were the words of the songs that he had loved so much and that had been a big part of our life together. During the day he would sometimes start to sing along to the music but often there would be tears in his eyes as he recalled the memories the songs brought back to him. I would ask him if a particular song had reminded him of the good times and he would look at me and just nod his head. He looked so sad and there would often be tears in his eyes; it was heartbreaking to see him like that.

Everything ran smoothly with the carers and we settled into a routine. However, I guess all good things come to an end as one morning a different carer turned up at a completely different time. I had not been notified and it caused problems because I would always get Bill up and sitting in his chair ready. It appeared that a new Manager had started at the Agency and one who thought it was more beneficial for the patient to have different carers and different visiting times rather than get used to the same one.

In my experience, I found this not to be the case as each carer would have a slightly different approach and a way of doing things. Bill would get agitated because the different routine was confusing for him and the different visiting times also threw out my routine. I was not happy until we had Andrew back again for a couple of mornings and he told me that he was actually leaving the Agency due to the way it was being run by the new Manager. However, he was moving to another Agency and had spoken to the Manager there and she was willing to take over Bill's care with Andrew remaining as his main carer. This worked fine for about six months and then once again a new Manager was brought in and the whole system was changed again. During this time some of the carers that we had were not up to the required standard and had a very poor command of the English language and so Bill would find it difficult to understand them and would get agitated. This caused further problems for me too. There appears to be a high turnover of Managers in the Care System with all of them having different ideas on how the system should be run. Why change a system that is working to something that is not. A good carer will know more about what works for the patient than those in the office do and so the system breaks down.

A change to private care: Finally, Andrew left to work for another man that he had also been caring for through the agency. He was to work on a full-time basis directly for him as part of his care team. However, he was concerned about the problems I was having with the Agency and offered to care for Bill privately too. If I agreed, he would come in to tend to Bill every morning before he started work at his new job and would call in on the way home to get him ready and into bed at the end of his day. I would pay him direct at the end of each week. It was a long day for him but he never failed to turn up with a smile on his face. We were fortunate that it worked well for us as we cared for Bill together. When he had his day off on a Sunday then I would cover his visit. We carried on like this and I must say he was a God send to us. I don't know what I would have done without him, he was always so professional. He didn't just care for Bill; he was also concerned with how I was and if I was coping alright.

As the care package was set up originally between the hospital and Social Services, I felt I should notify them of what I was doing as they would send me a bill every month for the care provided. When I rang their office to tell them what the new arrangements were, I was told that I couldn't do that but I assured them that I certainly could. The service that was being provided was not up to the standard I felt it should be and my priority was that my husband had the care he needed. Besides this, his care package was not subsidised and I was paying the full rate. I mentioned the saying that "he who pays the piper calls the tune". Conversation over and I looked forward to the new arrangement that couldn't have worked out better for us and everything ran smoothly once again. Well as smoothly as it could, depending on what stage of the dementia we were having to handle.

We used to occasionally go out for a pub lunch with his sister and brother-in-law which he used to enjoy but eating out after a while was to become a trauma for him, with the buzz of people talking around him, the clang of cutlery on plates, conversations of other people on surrounding tables he could no longer concentrate because of the noises in his ears. He would feel anxious and agitated. It was hard for us to understand as it was something we had often done and he had enjoyed going out but it was no longer feasible. It was just another thing that we had to stop.

One of the nurses that used to come in to see Bill told me that as part of her training for dementia care she went into 'the dementia bus' which had been kitted out inside to resemble a kitchen. The idea is for the carer to experience what life is like for someone with dementia and how they struggle to cope with the most simple instructions when other things are going on around them causing distraction. She told me that she was given headphones and dark glasses to put on before entering the bus. She found the jumble of noises and loud sounds that were coming through the headphones not only distracting but very distressing and making it difficult for her to understand the tasks she was being given.

Because of the dark glasses there appeared to be shadows in the room which can be a frightening experience for the dementia patient and with the addition of the loud noises she felt very confused and vulnerable but it helped her to understand how dementia affects the patient and the reasons for any unusual behaviour. She said she had found it very frightening and not something she would want to repeat. As she told me what the experience was like for her it helped me to understand what it was like for him. Another invaluable lesson learned that helped me cope with the problems that I was facing. Without this knowledge, I would have had no idea how an accumulation of various noises could affect him.

I remember one time when Alison visited from Spain, she stayed with him while I went for a dental appointment. When I got back, she said he had been very agitated and was asking for me. Her son who she hadn't seen for a while had called in to see her. Naturally, they were having a catch-up chat but because Bill was unable to follow the conversation it was just a babble of noise to him that he couldn't understand. When I asked him if he was ok, he said he wanted all these foreign people to go away and to leave him alone.

Vision perception: He then started to have problems with vision perception and distinguishing colours became a problem. For instance, when he came downstairs, he would reach the bottom step and would go no further. When I asked him what was wrong, he said he couldn't move off the bottom step because he would fall through the hole in the floor. When I said there was no hole, he pointed to the door mat. It was grey but against the laminate flooring he just saw it as a hole in the floor. I would move it out of the way and he then felt he was able to step down safely. Other days he saw it as a puddle of water and didn't want to get his feet wet. I eventually had to move it away from the door altogether and so no more problems.

One day I could hear him talking and went upstairs to see if he was ok. He was leaning forward in his chair with his hands on his knees and looking at the end of the bed. He turned to look at me as I entered the room, he had a big smile on his face and pointed to two of his pals that had called in to see him and were sitting on the end of the bed. He said he was having a good chat with them. There was of course nobody there but, in his mind, they were recalling the old days and reliving some of their memories. Why would I spoil that for him by telling him there was no-one there. He was happy with the company he thought he was in. The way I saw it, it was no different to a young child having an imaginary friend. If it made him happy then so was I.

On another occasion he was dozing on the settee with a knitted Aran blanket over his knees that kept his legs warm. With his vascular problems his legs were always cold. The cover had a narrow fur trim at each end. He woke up, looked down and started to stroke the fur; he wanted to know where the little kitten had come from that was sitting on his knee. I touched the fur and remarked how soft it was and said, "for a minute I thought that was a little kitten too but look Bill, it's the trim on the edge of your wool blanket." I smiled at him and he was happy with the explanation. I let him think that I also had thought it was a kitten at first. I knew what worked for him and so this is how I dealt with these situations by letting him think that I was also seeing what he saw and in that way he was content.

He often saw things that weren't there. In another instance he pointed to the armchair and asked who was the little girl that was sitting there. The biggest mistake that I found you can make in this situation, is to say that there isn't anyone sitting there. This would just get him angry and even more confused as quite clearly in his mind, there was someone sitting there. In this particular case there was a cushion on the chair. I just picked it up and said to him, 'look it's a cushion but you are right it just looks like a little girl, doesn't it?". He touched the cushion and smiled at me as I put it back on the chair. This might not work for everyone but it certainly worked for me.

There was one occasion I had left him sitting downstairs watching television, I had gone upstairs to clean the bedrooms. I heard him coming up the stairs and when he got to the landing, I asked him if he was alright. He said he was looking for his mum. I knew the minute the words came out of my mouth that I was giving him the wrong answer. I gently said to him, "your mum died Bill". It was the worst thing I could have said. He got really upset and said, "why did no-one tell me". His mother had died some 30 years earlier. I asked him would he like to sit in his chair and we could have a cup of tea together. By changing the subject in this way, he had forgotten already what I had said to him. I made us both a cup of tea and I sat down on the bed and started to chat to him. The next time he asked where his mum was, I said she had gone out shopping and would be back soon. He accepted that explanation and never asked again.

Restless nights: Another problem that we had to face were the restless nights as he moved into the middle stages of the disease. They were worrying times because he had his own room and although I would sleep lightly in case he needed me in the night, there were times when I woke and would go to check on him only to find he wasn't in bed. He would perhaps have been restless and would get up and go downstairs to see where I was. Fortunately, I had learnt in the early stages to lock the front door and hide the key just in case he tried to go out and wandered off which was a big fear of mine. I had heard of others doing this. I would find him sitting on the kitchen stool in the dark and when I asked him if he was ok, he would say he was looking for me and didn't know where I was. We would have a cup of tea together before I got him back to bed. It was about this time that, for his own safety, a camera was fitted in his bedroom that was connected to my iPad so that I could watch him wherever I was in the house. It was like having a new-born baby where you are always alert and seem to have one ear listening to every breathe that the baby takes in case it wakes up and needs you.

He had several falls during these times and I would often find him on the floor having either fallen out of bed or taken a tumble trying to get up out of bed. I would call Steve during the night to come and help me to lift him up and to settle him down again. He was too heavy for me to handle alone. It was fortunate that he lived just five minutes away. I don't know what I would have done without him living close by. Getting him up was not always easy as he didn't have the strength to help by pushing himself up and so he was a dead weight and it would take two of us to help him. Once we had got him up onto his feet Steve would lift him up and put him back into bed.

Sometimes, an ambulance had to be called and all credit to the paramedics that came out, they would check him over, make sure he was ok and comfortable before getting him back into his bed. On one of these call outs one of the paramedics asked me if I normally called my son out during the night and I said "yes, he lives less than five minutes away". He told me in future to always ring for an ambulance as I was disturbing my son's sleep and he then had to get up for work the next morning whilst they are already on duty and there to help when necessary. It also meant that they could check to make sure there were no other problems or signs of infection. They couldn't have been more helpful.

On one occasion though, it was early in the morning and I had found Bill on the floor between his bed and the wall. He had fallen from his bed and was lying in an awkward position. I could see blood on him but couldn't see where it was coming from so I called for an ambulance. When they came in, one of the paramedics went straight over to him, leaned down and said, "let's get you up from down there". Immediately, Bill was on the defensive and told him to go away and leave him alone. I was asked "is he always so tetchy with people that are trying to help him"? I said, "no, he is sick, he has dementia and he is frightened." The other medic asked me his name and then squatted down beside him, "introduced himself and said "hello Bill, would you like me to help you? Let's see if I can get you up onto the bed so that I can see where that blood is coming from." He nodded his head and while I continued to reassure him, the paramedic was able to lift him up, get him into his chair and assess him. He had taken the skin off his elbow and cut his arm in the fall. He had signs of an infection and would have to go to hospital.

The different attitude between the two paramedics on approaching Bill was a good example of the best way to deal with a dementia patient. The attitude of the first one was abrupt and had frightened him and he retaliated but accepted the more patient and friendlier approach of the second one. I was always mindful of the best approach depending on the mood he was in at the time. It was the only time he was uncooperative with a member of an ambulance crew.

Many a night I was woken by him sitting on my feet at the end of the bed. He had been to the toilet but had forgotten where his bedroom was even though it was right next door to the bathroom. I think also as he came out of the bathroom, he would vaguely remember the bedroom we had shared together throughout our married life but once there he no longer knew where he was or why he was there and so he would just sit down on the end of the bed, in the dark, wondering what to do next. I would ask him if he was ok and would he like to go back to bed. He would reply that he didn't know where his bed was.

Another night he woke me at 3.30am in a very agitated state telling me I had to get up as we needed to get packed because we had to be out of our room by 10.00am for the cleaner to come in. He said he had packed all his stuff, so he was ready to go. Fortunately, I was able to think quickly on my feet and I said we had time for a quick cup of tea before we left and brought him downstairs, sat him on the settee while I put the kettle on but within minutes of him sitting down, he was fast asleep. I went back upstairs to his room and found his wardrobe door wide open and completely empty. He had taken all his clothes out and folded them up on the bed ready for us to leave. He must have thought that we were on holiday and that we had to be out of our room before the next guests were due to arrive. I put everything back into the wardrobe and took a blanket down to cover him up and sat beside him as he slept until the morning. When he woke up, he had absolutely no recollection of what had gone on before. I got very little sleep at times like these but he needed me so I was always there for him.

Difficult mornings: As the disease went into yet another stage, there were times in the morning when Andrew arrived to get him up, that he didn't remember who he was. He would refuse to get out of bed and would shout and swear and tell him to go away. After much persuasion but without success Andrew would have to leave to go onto his main job. I would then try to do what Andrew had failed to do, through no fault of his own but then he would turn his anger onto me. I would retaliate and shout back at him but would then be riddled with guilt at some of the things I had said. I felt so ashamed of my reactions as this disease pushed me to the limits. I knew this wasn't his normal behaviour; he would also have forgotten that I had shouted back at him, probably within the first couple of minutes or even less but I never forgot and was filled with remorse. It was like living in a Jekyll & Hyde situation.

As hard as it was and for my own sanity I had to learn to walk away. I would make sure he was safe and then just leave him in bed, go downstairs and watch him on my iPad as he would pull the sheet over his face like he was shutting out the world and would go back to sleep. It was a gesture that I noticed him do many times when he was in hospital. I would have loved to have been able to do the same, but I couldn't in case he woke up and not being steady on his feet he could fall if he tried to get out of bed unaided and so as tired as I was, I would just sit and watch to make sure he was ok. I would wait until I saw him move and sit himself up on the side of the bed, usually a couple of hours later.

When I walked back into his room, he would be pleased to see me and casually say, 'morning', the same way he did every morning throughout our life together. He had no knowledge of his earlier behaviour and the upset he had caused. If he had of been in his right mind, he would have been devastated at what he was putting me through. I would ask him if he would like me to help him get washed and dressed and he would say "yes please, if you don't mind" and he would give me that smile that I knew so well. At times like this he would always thank me for helping him.

I realised eventually that during these times of anger not only did he not know who Andrew was, I don't believe he knew who I was either. It was like a blackness momentarily clouded his vision and so he would be frightened. It was as if we were two strangers that had come in and invaded his space and he felt vulnerable. On these days it meant he was having breakfast when others would be having their lunch; but did that really matter? He was the priority and I had to go along with whatever was easier for him but also what became easier for me too.

This turned out to be the best option as I found another way of handling the situation and so the shouting stopped and life became just that little bit easier for both of us and it was another hurdle overcome. When Andrew returned in the evening he would squat down besides Bill's chair, put his hand on his arm and would quietly ask him if he knew who he was. Bill would give his usual reply, "I think so, but I don't know your name" as soon as he was told it was Andrew, he would grab hold of his hand with both of his and look up at him and smile.

This was one of the hardest and most frustrating periods to go through and I was at my wits end but I knew this wasn't the real Bill, the Bill that I had loved with all of my heart, for so many years. This was the outcome of the awful disease that had taken over and was slowly destroying his brain. Don't let anyone tell you that dementia is a disease where the person just forgets things. It is so much more than that. To understand it fully you need to live with it 24 hours a day, 7 days a week. It was the hardest thing I've ever had to do in my life.

Fortunately, the restless nights diminished as the disease progressed but they were then replaced by other problems. The lack of sleep and sheer exhaustion caught up with me as he began to move into yet another stage of dementia.

One Sunday when it was Andrew's day off. I was getting Bill washed and dressed in the bathroom and as I was bending down to put his socks on, I caught his foot. He shouted and told me to be more careful and that he was going to ring the Agency to tell them I wasn't properly trained. He said to me, "you call yourself a carer"? I said "no, I'm not a carer, I'm your wife who is just trying to do her best for you". At the time I was on my knees and about to stand up. It didn't matter what mood he was in at the time whenever he saw me bending down and was about to get up, he would automatically help me get to my feet.

Once Bill was settled into his chair in the mornings he would sit and listen to his music which we had playing 24 hours a day, sometimes singing along and others just moving his index finger in time to the music. At night I would turn the sound down but just enough for him to hear so that if he woke up during the night he would know where he was, not be frightened and know that he was safe. It was during these times that he was at his happiest.

Hallucinations: Another time I was reading a book and Bill was sitting in the conservatory, it was a sunny day and he was listening to his music. I heard him talking so I got up and went to see if he was ok. He was sitting on the settee but was looking across at a chair opposite him. On the chair was a knitted doll that was dressed as a gardener, it was about 18 inches high and he appeared to be talking to it. When I asked him if he was alright, he said he was talking to His Holiness, the Pope. I remembered him telling me once that when he worked in the convent all those years ago and just 14, there was a young lad working there who was being treated badly and he would often see him crying. He complained to someone about it and was told to mind his own business and to get on with his work but it was something that had always bothered him and so he was telling the Pope about it and was hoping that he would be able to put things right. How strange that he should remember that incident more than 70 years later.

A little while afterwards he came into the room where I was and sat in an armchair and started talking, completely unaware that I was sitting close by. He was saying, as if to someone that I couldn't see, that he was going out to meet his mates for a drink and how they would always be pleased to see him. When he walked into the bar they would say, "here comes Bill, he's always good for a song or two." I found this very strange as apart from singing along with his music or in my ear when we were courting many years ago as we danced cheek to cheek, I had never ever heard of him singing and certainly not in a bar or indeed in front of other people. Obviously, something in his imagination or was it like having a dream but actually being awake. As I listened to him, I felt the tears running down my cheek. It was so sad to see him drift off into this other world.

Another time as we were sitting together watching television one evening, he suddenly said, "what is he doing out there looking in at us?" He was angry and started swearing. When I asked him who it was, he said "his father was looking through the conservatory window at us." He hadn't seen his father since he was 8 years old when he had left the family home more than 70 years before. I looked towards the conservatory and saw that the reflection from the television screen was reflecting onto the half open glass door of the living room and was then reflecting back onto the conservatory window. I closed the door and the reflection disappeared. I told him there was no-one there and that it was just a reflection but he wasn't convinced and he thought that he was still out there.

One night I was woken by him shouting out and swearing "get out of my house, you *bastard*" I looked at the clock, it was 3.00am, I got up and pushed open the door to his room that was ajar and found him sitting on the edge of the bed. There was always a small dimmer light on in his bedroom in case he woke up. I asked him what was wrong and he pointed to the door I had just opened and he said, "get that *bastard* out of here". I switched the main light on and closed the door back over. What he was looking at was his dressing gown hanging up behind the door. In the half-light he saw it as the figure of a man just another incident of vision perception in the dim lighting. I calmed him down and said he had been dreaming and asked him would he like a cup of tea so that he could go back to sleep again. He said he would and wanted to listen to his music. I helped him up to sit in his chair, put the music on and made him a cup of tea. I sat with him while he drank it and listened to the music.

He said he was tired and wanted to go back to bed. I turned the big light out, left the dimmer on and his music turned low. The dressing gown was taken off the hook behind the door and put into the bathroom and all was peaceful once again and I was able to go back to bed myself knowing that my alarm would be going off in less than an hour for me to get up. When Andrew called the next morning, I explained that he had had a bad night and that I was going let him sleep and I would get him washed and dressed when he woke up. He would usually go up to check on him and would stay and chat with me for a while.

These middle stages of the disease I found were the most difficult, I never knew what was going to come next. Every day was different and I had to find ways of calming him down and making sure he felt safe and secure. When he had outbursts, it was usually because he was afraid, didn't know his surroundings and was feeling vulnerable. One good thing was that he was never violent like some people are who are struck down with this disease, his outbursts were all verbal.

Mobility: Having dementia but with mobility in some ways is easier because it does mean that the patient is able to move around the house unaided and able to spend some time in the fresh air in and around the garden. I guess that it would also be easier to take them out without the worry of falls but then you have the problem if left alone they can wander off, leave the house and then forget where they are, get lost and perhaps step out onto a busy road without looking so that in itself, is a dangerous situation but a common symptom of the disease.

Bill's mobility was poor with some days worse than others, so without our own transport it was difficult getting on and off buses with a wheelchair because of the risk of falls. Once we did get out, things would be fine. We would stop for a coffee and watch the world go by but then when we got back home, he would become confused and want to know whose house we were in. The thing I found strange was that although he didn't recognise the house that we had lived in for more than 45 years, if I asked him what his address was, he was able to say it without even thinking about it. He always knew his date of birth and his national insurance number off by heart too. I certainly didn't know mine. When asking him his age though he would always say he was 60 even though by this stage he was in his early 80s. Maybe this was because we had organized a surprise birthday party for him when he was 60 with his family coming from Ireland and as it was a special time for him, had stayed in his memory. What a mystery the workings of the mind are!

He was always at risk of falls which were often due to an infection that would affect his mobility and he would be admitted to hospital. Some of the falls were during the night when he was still able to get up unaided, to go to the toilet.

He would be ok getting there but then having been on his feet for a little while he would take a tumble on the way back. There were many nights when I would only get 3-4 hours sleep as I would lie awake listening out for him.

There were times when he would fall out of bed or on trying to get up but would just lie there. When I got up in the morning, I would find him lying on the floor and I'd ask him why he hadn't called out to me for help, he would say he didn't want to disturb me. It was difficult for me to lift him as he was a dead weight and he couldn't help by pushing himself up either. Another time he would help me by sliding himself on the floor over towards his chair and then managing to get up onto his knees and I would then be able to get him up onto his feet and seated in the chair. When he was cooperative, he would always try to help me. If I was down on my hands and knees putting his socks or shoes on as soon as I went to get up, he would put his hand under my elbow to help me. At times like this he would always thank me for whatever it was I was doing for him.

However, despite the mobility problems there were three occasions when he did manage to wander off while I was out of sight in the garden. Fortunately, on one of these occasions I saw him further up the road and ran after him, frightened to call out because he had no stick to steady himself and was in his slippers. When I reached him, I just touched his arm to let him know I was there and he said, "there you are I'm just going home". He was holding in his hand a small photo frame with a picture of our grandchildren when they were young, a couple of his CDs that he had taken out of the rack and some coasters in his pocket; his possessions he told me that he needed to take with him in case somebody stole them. I suggested we go back to get his coat and so that he could put his shoes on. As we turned around, he pointed down the road and said, "there's my house that's where I live." More than happy then to come back in and to sit down with a cup of tea.

Another time he was very agitated and confused and said he was going home. Even with the lack of mobility he managed to get past me and out of the front door. It was raining heavily, he had no coat on, was in slippers and no stick to support him. I couldn't believe how quickly he was able to move. It was like he found an inner strength, so desperate was he to get home. I had to stop to pick up his coat and walking stick and make sure I had the keys so that I could shut the front door. He had got round the corner and across a small road and was walking down towards the Heath. I called out to him to come back but he just turned round, shouted at me, and said he was going home to his family. He was very agitated but when I got beside him, I quietly told him he was going the wrong way. When he turned around, he saw the flats at the top of the road and then knew where he was. I just said to him, "it's cold and wet, let's go home together." He was still very agitated and confused and so Steve came down to chat with him and said that if he wanted to go home then he would take him. He put his coat on and took him out to the car and drove him around the streets on the estate. He soon began to recognise the area and was happy then when they pulled up outside the house, he came back inside, happy and content that he really was home in his own house.

I just had to learn to cope with these difficult situations and believe me everyone one was different. Although it's not easy, it's a case of going along with them and then trying to distract them whilst trying to remain calm yourself. Once they are calm again it's easier to just chat away like everything is normal and they feel safe again. Although I found these experiences frightening, how much worse must it have been for him not knowing where he was.

Our wedding anniversary: On our wedding anniversary, eight months before he died, I gave him a card and wished him a happy anniversary, all I got was that blank stare that I had seen so many times before. I decided to get out one of our wedding photographs and asked him if he knew who the couple were in the picture. He looked at it for a long time with no reaction and no recognition, then said he thought the man looked a bit like his brother. When I asked him if he knew the lady in the picture, he said he had never seen her before but it wasn't just me that he didn't know, when I got him to look in the mirror after having a haircut, he didn't know who the person was looking back at him. Later that day as we sat on the settee together, he asked me if I could tell him what happened when we got married as he couldn't remember but he knew that I was his wife. If only dementia would allow those special times to remain in the memory it would be such a comfort to the patient to be able to recall the happy times in their life.

The dementia moves to yet another stage: Fortunately, as the disease progressed, he became calmer and the restlessness eased as he went into yet another stage but for me it just meant another set of problems that I would have to face. He became more reliant on me and was forgetting how to do the most simple things for himself. When I put his dinner in front of him, he would just sit and look at it and look at the knife and fork at the side of his plate. I would ask him would he like me to cut up his meat and he would nod but would look vague. He watched what I was doing and when I put some food onto the fork and put it into his hand with the knife it was like he suddenly remembered how to use them but he soon forgot again and it wasn't long before they were replaced with a spoon and easier meals for him to handle. It was such a simple thing, a skill that a toddler learns from his mother as he advances from using a spoon to a knife and fork but now it was like he was progressing backwards and reverting to the use of a spoon rather than the knife and fork.

One hot summer day, I had done the washing, ironing, housework and been out in the garden to cut the grass. I stopped for a rest and made a cup of tea for both of us. I was sitting on the end of his bed, he was looking me up and down and then he suddenly said, quite seriously, "you need to smarten yourself up, you're letting yourself go." I had an old pair of jeans on as I had been gardening and a t-shirt. I was really hot; my hair was a mess and I had been on my feet for almost 5 hours without a break. He didn't realise just how much I had to do and this would not have been his normal behaviour had he not been ill. Another morning, after having a shower and getting dressed I could go into his room and wake him up with a cup of tea. He would look at me, smile and say, "you look nice today". I never knew what sort of mood I would find him in.

There was one morning I went into his room to get his breakfast dishes and as I picked up his cereal bowl, I accidently knocked his mug over that still had tea in it and it spilt all over the floor. I swore and used the 'F' word, a word

I hate and never use but it was just something else I had to clean up. Bill looked at me and said "don't you dare use that sort of language in front of me" I looked up at him and said, "seriously, and who do you think taught me that sort of language" realising what he had said he looked at me and smiled and we both saw the funny side of it. I swore out of frustration and I was just so tired.

The vision perception got worse and different colours seemed to have a big impact in other ways. I remember in the later stages when one morning I put his breakfast in front of him and went out of the room to do a few other jobs. Usually, he would pick up the spoon straight away and start eating but five minutes later when I looked in on him, I saw that he was just sitting there looking at the plate. He had always loved porridge and he usually had it every morning as it was easy for him to digest but on this particular morning, he was just sitting looking at it. I asked him if he didn't want his breakfast and he said he hadn't been given any. I went over to him, picked up the spoon and filled it with porridge and held it to his mouth. Once he had tasted it, I put the spoon into his hand and guided it towards the plate, realising there was food there, he carried on eating. Looking back on it now, I think the problem was he couldn't distinguish the porridge from the white plate. I then remembered reading about the problems with vision perception and that it is hard to distinguish mashed potato on a white plate. The use of a coloured plate made all the difference. I tried to imagine things as he saw them but it was difficult and that is why I read up on all I could on the subject of dementia and found that by reading other peoples' experiences and how they handled them meant I could be one step ahead of the game a lot of the time but not all of the time.

Bill was admitted to hospital on several occasions due to various infections. On being discharged he would have visits from the hospital Home Care team, a nurse and physiotherapist, for the first 7 days. Each day they would check his blood pressure, temperature, blood sugars and do blood tests. The physio, with the help of the nurse would do leg exercises and work on improving his mobility. Later that evening I would get a call from one of the hospital doctors giving me the results of the various tests that had been carried out on him. I didn't know this service existed as I had not heard of anyone having it before. Apparently, it was something that our local Medical Centre paid into. It was certainly a good service and helped to get him back on his feet. Unfortunately, at that time it was a service not available in all areas, hopefully this is no longer the case. In Bill's case it meant that he got one to one care from hospital staff whilst settled in his own home amid familiar surroundings. He would not have got the same care had he have still been in hospital.

Just before his last Christmas, Bill wasn't too well, his mobility was poor and so I did a urine test which indicated a possible infection. I rang the surgery asking for a home visit. When the doctor came in, he asked Bill if it was alright if he called him William; his immediate reaction was 'no'. The doctor looked puzzled as he turned to me. I said everyone calls him Bill and that he would be alright if he called him that. He agreed that he had an infection but said he didn't want him admitted to hospital over the Christmas period but as the surgery would be closed for several days over the holidays he would refer him, if I agreed, to the hospital Home Care Team, who would come in each day to check on him. This put my mind at rest knowing that medical attention would be available should it be needed.

He often had falls resulting in cuts and bruises that needed attention. The doctor would pass instructions to the District Nurses to come in daily to dress his wounds. Without this help and support I don't think I could have managed. I was lucky that we had a good Medical Centre.

It was during one of the visits by the Home Care Team that he had a blip. A physio had come in with a nurse and Bill had been chatting to them with no problems, the physio was about to start his leg exercises and the nurse had put her glasses on and was updating the medical records in his care file. He suddenly started shouting at her and told her to get out of his house. The physio touched his arm and said that she was his nurse and was there to help him. I realised immediately what had happened, his reaction came as she put on her glasses which made her look different. I told them what I thought had caused his reaction and she took them off again and he calmed down but his outburst had upset her. However, when they went to leave and she said goodbye to him, he said to her, with no prompting, 'I think I owe you an apology, I'm very sorry' he was full of remorse. She smiled, put her hand on his shoulder and kissed him on the cheek.

On another occasion a similar thing happened with one of the district nurses who often came in to treat him. One minute he was fine and chatting to her and then suddenly he started shouting and accused her of being a Nazi spy and told her she had to leave. Where did that come from? Maybe from watching too many WW2 films over the years, who knows? These incidents occurred as the disease progressed. Just like Jekyll & Hyde, one minute he would be fine and pleasant and then he would have one of these outbursts. Fortunately, they were few and far between but so difficult to understand what triggered them off. What was happening to his brain and what caused these reactions? I would do my best to distract him with something else to calm him down. It wasn't always easy though.

I am exhausted and beginning to struggle: In May 2018 I celebrated my 80th birthday, Alison came over from Spain to spend a few days with us but as Bill was now in the later stages of the disease there were just a few members of the family here. He sat in the conservatory while most of us were in the garden. He couldn't understand what was going on and these gatherings were beginning to get too much for him. Feeling both mentally and physically exhausted at that time I wondered just how much longer I could carry on without a break. I hadn't mentioned this to the family as I didn't want them to worry about me too but on opening one of my birthday presents the news of a break came in the most unexpected way.

I was a big fan of Andrea Bocelli and Dave and Debby had obtained tickets and were to take me to see him in concert in Tuscany in July. It was something that was always on my bucket list but something I thought could never be achieved. When I got over the initial surprise, I realised it would be impossible for me to go. What about Bill? There was no way I could leave him. I was assured that arrangements had been made for Alison to come back and stay with him so that I could have this break and Steve would be around to back her up and to help if there were any problems. Andrew would continue to come in each day to get him up in the mornings and put him to bed at night. It was to be for a long weekend, leaving Friday morning and arriving home on Monday evening. I was so excited but still very concerned about being away from home. I kissed him goodnight when he went to bed on Thursday evening and when I returned home on the Monday evening he was in bed and I went in and said goodnight to him. I don't think he was even aware that I had been away. Alison said he hadn't been too well for the past couple of days but I said I would see how he was the next morning and if he was no better would call the doctor. She was booked on the first flight out of Gatwick on Tuesday morning. I can never ever thank my children enough for enabling me to have that break, without it I don't know how I would have got through the next few months.

Another infection and a hospital stay: When Andrew came in the next morning, we discussed how Bill was and he suggested I give it another day and if he was no better to get medical advice. The next morning his mobility was very poor and he had all the signs of yet another infection and so I rang for an ambulance. Andrew arrived while the paramedics were checking on Bill and as he needed to go to hospital, they let him get Bill washed and dressed while they wrote up their notes.

I felt so guilty that I had been away for those few days but had I have been here it would have made no difference he would still have gone down with an infection. Whilst he was in A&E, they took blood samples and he had chest x-rays. From the tests that were carried out it was confirmed that he had an infection but they could not discover what the infection was or where it was but they suspected sepsis and so he was to be admitted to an assessment ward. It was a very busy ward with nurses and doctors rushing in and out. By this time, it was mid-afternoon and we had been at the hospital since early morning. Bill was dozing in and out of sleep and looked very flushed. I didn't like the look of him and called a nurse. I told her that he was diabetic and had not had anything to eat that morning as the ambulance had brought him in before he had had any breakfast. She went off to get him something sweet to eat but he was getting very agitated and wouldn't take the food that was offered. As he was not a good colour, she got a more senior nurse to take a look at him. She pricked his finger to do a blood test and found his blood sugar was down to 4 which was far too low. They tried to squeeze a jelly substance from a tube into his mouth but by this time he was fighting them off. Dave who had just arrived to see him suggested that he might accept it from me and so he calmed him and held him still while I squeezed the contents of the tube into his mouth. It did the trick and soon started to take effect. They had found a bed for him in one of the wards but decided he was not well enough to be moved and so he was kept in the assessment ward overnight and moved the next morning when his condition had stabilised.

Over the next couple of days his condition had improved slightly but he still had the infection. His bed had already been moved a couple of times and he was now in a single ward. It was mid-summer and it was very hot, no air conditioning in the hospital and so they had put a fan in his room. When we went in that evening he was sitting up in bed and was able to chat to us. He seemed to be a lot better and there was no confusion. We spent a couple of hours with him until the bell rang indicating that visiting hours were over but he didn't want us to leave. I said we would stay just a little longer or until we were thrown out. He was happy with that, he looked at me and said, "I love you". I kissed him on the cheek and said "I love you too" but we really have to go now but I'll come in to see you tomorrow.

The next day he had been moved again, this time to the floor above but he was still in a single ward. He was sitting up in bed listening to the music on the hospital radio and he seemed a lot better. He was chatting away and seemed quite happy and so I was expecting him to be discharged fairly soon. He had been in the hospital for two weeks, the longest stay so far.

He is moved to a rehabilitation ward: The following morning, I got a call to say that he was being moved yet again, this time into a rehabilitation ward so that he could have physio to get him mobile before discharging him. I was told the name of the ward where I would find him when I visited that afternoon. On arriving at the hospital, I had trouble finding the ward and had to ask for directions. I was told the ward was not in the main hospital but in another building in the hospital grounds and that it was 'a care for the elderly' ward. When I finally found the ward that he was in, he was like a different person from the one I had visited the previous day. As I went over to kiss him, he just turned away from me, he looked hurt and the look on his face said, 'it was you who put me in here'. I was so shocked and could not believe the change in him in just 24 hours. He was going backwards.

A nurse came in and was putting his medication in a cupboard on the wall and told me his insulin was in the fridge. When I told her that he had been off insulin for more than two years, she said "oh! well they must have put him back on it then". I wanted to know why I had not been informed as I was at the hospital every day for 5 hours or more. She said she didn't know and she was just following instructions. He wanted to come home with me and I think he thought that it was me that was making him stay there.

It was such a depressing ward; it was dull and dismal and completely different to the main hospital. It looked like it needed a complete refurbishment. The curtains were hanging off of a broken curtain rail and the television didn't work. There were four beds in the ward. The patient in the bed opposite just spent the time staring at Bill so it was a little unnerving for him. He had Parkinson's with dementia and was bed bound. The man in the next bed to him was dressed in day clothes and wanted to know where the door was to get out. He was worried that he didn't have his card to get money out of the machine for his fare home. He never sat still and was up and down the corridor all the time until a nurse would bring him back into the ward. The other patient who was in the next bed to Bill kept getting out of bed, taking his gown off and wandering around without his clothes on and opening the medical waste bins and putting his hands inside. There were no signs of any medical staff. Within just a couple of hours I was beginning to feel depressed just by being there. I could only imagine what it was like for him. I was the only visitor in the ward and it was like the patients had just been dumped there and forgotten about. It was such an awful place that I can only describe as 'God's waiting room' and so sad to see. Bill started to go downhill rapidly and I was not happy that he had been moved into such a depressing environment and knew he would be much better off at home where he would have one-to-one care and be in surroundings that were familiar to him and with his music to calm him.

When I went in to see him the next day, he was in a terrible state. It was 5.00pm and he was still in bed; he hadn't been washed and his hair was in a mess. His arms and the backs of his hands were covered in cuts and bruises and the rails at the sides of his bed were up. When I asked what had happened to him, I was told that he did it to himself trying to get out of bed. He had not done that during the previous two weeks that he had been in hospital nor had the rails at the sides of the bed been up either. So, what had changed? I had my thoughts on this but I felt helpless and I didn't want to cause a fuss in front of him. The ward was completely run by Agency staff and in the main I never saw the same nurse twice during his time there. The standard of care was very poor and so different to what he had received in the main hospital building. There never seemed to be a responsible person in charge and if there was, they never appeared to be available whilst I was there. I washed and shaved him myself and combed his hair but I was worried about the cuts and bruises to his arms. Whenever I visited him on the following days he was always lying in bed in the same sorry state. He was supposed to be having physiotherapy ready to be discharged and got out of bed each day to sit in a chair but no-one was attending to him and he certainly wasn't getting any physio. I asked why he hadn't been out of bed since moving to the ward and was told they weren't allowed to get a patient out of bed unless the physiotherapist had said they could.

Whenever I asked questions, I was told I had to ask the nurse who did the medications. When she came into the ward and I asked her, she was so rude and kept her back to me all the time and wouldn't even look at me. I asked her if I could speak to a doctor, I was told there wasn't one available. I asked when the Consultant, whose name was on the wall above his bed, would be available; she didn't know. I never noticed that Dave had come into the ward as I was speaking to her, but he had noticed her attitude and the state his dad was in. I heard him say, "I'll be back in a minute mum". When he came back, he said he had been out to complain about the treatment his dad was receiving and that we wanted him discharged so that we could take him home where he would be better cared for. We felt he was being neglected. He was given the telephone number of a doctor and told to ring her the next morning. Dave made the call to the lady doctor and told her that we were not happy with how he was being treated and that we wanted him discharged into our care and to take him home immediately. She said although he wasn't her patient, she would look into our complaint and asked what time I would be visiting that afternoon so that she could have a chat with me and said she would make a point of coming in to see me. What a difference when I arrived that afternoon, Bill had been shaved and washed, his hair was combed, he was sitting in his chair and for the first time since he had been moved there, smiled and was pleased to see me. On the previous days he would turn his face away from me when I went in to see him. I think he blamed me for the situation he was in and how he was being treated. The doctor came in while I was there and said she had personally got him out of bed with help from a nurse and he had managed to walk around the bed with her help. Where were the physios who were actually based in the same building? She asked Bill if he would mind if she took me into her office to talk with me. He was happy for that to happen and she left a young nurse sitting with him and encouraging him to eat his lunch.

Apparently, she was a GP that went into the hospital to help. I told her that when I arrived to see him just after he had been moved to the ward a nurse, who was putting his medication in the cupboard on the wall close to his bed, told me that his insulin was in the fridge. I asked her why he had been put back on it as he had been off it for several years. She said he shouldn't be on it and that they must be reading from old notes. She looked up his records on the computer and said it had been stopped. She asked me various questions about his general state of health before he had been admitted to hospital and whether anyone had spoken to me about a DNR. No-one had and so she asked if Bill was in his right mind, how he would he feel about it. I said that if he was in his right mind, feeling as he was and able to make that decision himself, he would not want to be resuscitated especially at his age and in his present condition.

I had heard that ribs can be broken when being resuscitated especially in someone who was as frail as he was. She said that if he needed to be resuscitated and they were able to bring him back, then his condition would be far worse than it was at present. She asked how the rest of his family would feel about a DNR; I didn't need to ask them I knew how they felt, they would feel the same way as I did and did not want to see him suffer. She filled in the form and got me to sign it, gave me a copy for his file at home that was kept up to date by the District Nurses that visited. It was a Thursday when I saw her and it was to be Bill's 84th birthday on the Saturday and I wanted him home for that. However, she wanted to keep him in over the weekend so that she could get the physios to work on his mobility but that she would see that he was discharged into my care on the following Monday. She was so kind and it helped that she was English so I could get my point across to her and she was sympathetic to our concerns as a family.

All the time Bill was in this ward I only saw one young nurse in the whole unit that was English speaking and appeared to be the only properly trained dementia nurse but she was not there every day. I have no problem with nurses or medical staff from other countries providing they are caring and properly trained to our standards but in this ward that didn't appear to be the case. The ward was completely run by agency staff that all appeared to have a very poor command of the English language and many of them were rude with bad attitudes. It seemed to me that they were general 'care workers' and not very good ones at that rather than properly trained medical staff. I found the staff in the other wards of the main hospital that he had been in very helpful, kind and polite.

I mentioned to the doctor what a bad environment this ward was for dementia patients and that the television didn't work, that there was nothing to keep them occupied and they were just being left to their own devices. If they were left in this environment for any length of time, then they would rapidly go downhill. From my own experience in caring for Bill, I said some music quietly playing in the background would have made all the difference but she said they are not allowed to have music on the wards. A decision obviously made by someone with no knowledge of what works for a lot of dementia patients. What I felt would have helped was to have had some calming music playing softly in the background. After all patients in the main medical wards have the opportunity of listening to music via the hospital radio and with the aid of earphones but there was nothing for the patients in this ward.

During the times I sat with him, I could hear people from other wards in this building screaming or calling out for help. It was very upsetting. I visited every day and would sit with Bill for 4 or 5 hours and during that time I never saw any other visitors. It was quite obvious that it was a dementia ward and not the best place for him to be in. I couldn't wait to get him out of there.

I made up my mind then that if he got another infection, I would refuse to let him go into hospital again and I had this put on his medical records. There was no point in him being hospitalised as the medication they gave him could be given at home just as easily and I could care for him better with the help of his Carer, who came in twice a day, the doctors at our Medical Centre and the District Nurses who were all very good and catered adequately for his needs.

The only bad experience that we had ever come across within the National Health Service over the years that he had needed treatment, was in this unit for the elderly. I felt strongly that it needed to be either closed down or certainly refurbished and provided with properly trained nursing staff. There was nothing to stimulate the patients and I felt they were being neglected. They might be elderly, suffering from some form of dementia and difficult to handle which I know from my own experience but above all they are human beings and should be cared for in the same way as any other patient. I can't believe that as a society we allow our elderly to be treated in such an inhumane manner.

Discharge from hospital: On the following Monday the hospital rang to say Bill was being discharged and would be coming home by hospital transport that afternoon. Whilst he was in hospital, I had painted the walls in his bedroom white so that it was nice and bright for him. It was comfortable and cosy and I already had his music softly playing in the background. I couldn't wait to have him back where he belonged. When the ambulance arrived there were the two ambulance girls and two young girls from the physio department who wanted to assess him walking up the stairs. Really! It was a bit late for that and this should have been done before he left the hospital but most days in that last week, they hadn't even bothered to get him out of bed. He couldn't stand on his own unaided, let alone walk up the stairs, due to not having the necessary physio whilst he was in their care and there was no excuse for that as the physio department was housed in the same building. I was so shocked at the state of him, it looked like he hadn't been washed or his hair combed. He was still in a hospital gown with plasters on his arms that were still badly bruised. When I asked why he wasn't dressed as I had taken clothes in for him, I was told he wouldn't let anyone dress him but it looked as if nobody had even bothered to try. As far as I was concerned this was down to the poor standard of care that the patients were receiving in this 'care for the elderly' ward.

When our front door is opened wide, as it was to get the wheelchair in, it blocks the stairs. The two physios were trying to get him out of the wheelchair so that he could stand up but he was just too weak and to be quite honest they didn't seem to know what they were doing. In the end it was the two ambulance girls who took over and helped him. They transferred him to another chair from the ambulance and carried him up the stairs and got him seated in his chair in the bedroom. I don't know how we would have managed without them. The Ambulance Service could not be faulted.

The first thing I did when they left was to make him a little more comfortable, I gently washed his face, combed his hair and turned his music up. He looked at me with tears in his eyes as he looked around his bedroom, he grabbed my hand and thanked me. It broke my heart to see him like this. I sat beside him and held him in my arms, there was no way he would be away from me again. I made us both a cup of tea and gave him some biscuits and sat with him until Andrew came. I had rung him earlier and said he was home and that he was still in a hospital gown and was in a sorry state. He told me not to worry and that when he came in, he would give him a good washdown and put him in his pyjamas, make him comfortable and get him into bed. When he arrived, he bent down beside Bill and put his hand gently on his knee. He said, "do you know who I am Bill?" He replied, "I think so but I don't know your name." He said, "I'm Andrew". The tears filled Bill's eyes again as he remembered him, he grabbed hold of Andrew's hand with both of his and said, "thank you." I was so grateful for his kindness and how he treated Bill. He looked a different person when he was washed and changed and ready for bed. I had taken photos of him on his discharge from hospital to show our children and what he looked like after Andrew's care. I was so disgusted at how he was discharged from hospital and thinking back on it now, I know I should have made a formal complaint but my priority at that time was caring for Bill and getting him over the awful experience of his stay on the ward for the elderly. He had been through enough.

I know there is a shortage of nurses and medical staff in the NHS and I can understand how that causes problems but using Agency staff of such a low standard, in my opinion, is not the best idea and probably costs the NHS more money in the long run. We need to put money into the system and train our own nurses. As I said earlier, I have no problem with using overseas nursing staff providing they have the necessary qualifications that meet up with our standards and a good command of the English language especially when they are treating the elderly who are frightened and vulnerable. In our experience we found the nurses especially from the Philippines and many other countries very kind and compassionate, with a good command of English and excellent nursing skills and couldn't fault them in any way.

It was because of this experience that I stipulated no more hospital admissions and in future, any infections were to be treated at home under the care of our GP and Medical Centre, which was our wish as a family.

I have absolutely no complaint about the main hospital wards where he was treated with compassion or any part of the NHS system that was involved with his care over the years and cannot sing their praises highly enough. I cannot fault the doctors and staff at our local Medical Centre where I was always able to speak to a doctor if I had any concerns and could aways get a doctor to come out to see him if I was worried about anything.

The District Nurses had been notified that he had been discharged and that the wounds on his arms needed to be dressed daily. He was now back in our care and I was going to make sure that is where he was going to stay.

The Community Matron: who was based at the hospital, was notified of his discharge and anything that was needed for his care at home she would arrange by liaising with the surgery and District Nurses. A few days later she called in to introduce herself and to have a chat with both Bill and myself. Her job, although based at the hospital, seemed to entail working in the community to enable people like him to stay in their own homes, where possible, with the necessary help rather than be admitted to Hospital or moved into a Care Home.

When she came downstairs to talk with me, she said she would notify the Hospice and asked had we got any plans for his 'end of life' care. This really upset me and I said I didn't know that he was at that stage. She reassured me that it was because we had stipulated no further hospital stays that we needed to get a plan sorted for his medical records.

By notifying the Hospice it also meant she could get any equipment that he might require through them and much quicker than if she went through the normal hospital channels. She suggested that it might help to get him a virtual Hospice bed with a special mattress for his comfort and to stop him getting bed sores. In this way it meant he would come under the Hospice and their care should the need arise.

She helped me by filling in a form for his medical records with details of what care he might need in the coming months. As we had said 'no' to further hospital stays, she asked if his condition got too bad that he could no longer be treated at home, would we be happy for him to spend his final days in the Hospice and who he would want with him when that time came. I agreed to this and for his family to be with him. She said if I was happy with everything then she would notify the Hospice and arrange for a bed to be delivered. It was delivered the next day.

Once the Hospice bed had been delivered one of their therapists came in to visit Bill to assess his situation and to advise me as to what help was available from them. If I had any concerns between the hours of 6.00pm and 8.00am then I could contact them and speak to one of their nurses. This meant that between our Medical Centre, District Nurses and the Community Matron any medical problems were covered without the necessity of a hospital stay.

Once he was home and in our care, he gradually settled down and was always pleased to see any of the family when they came to visit. As his mobility improved over the next few weeks, there were days, with help, that he was still able to come downstairs and sit in the conservatory where he could look out onto the garden while listening to his music. He enjoyed those times and it was his favourite place to be especially on a bright sunny day. We would have our meal together in the evening and Andrew would help him back upstairs when he came in to get him ready for bed.

One afternoon we were sitting on the settee together watching television when he suddenly asked me if I would sit next to him. I said "I'm already sitting next to you" but he wanted me to sit closer to him as there was a gap of about 6 inches between us and so I moved closer so that our knees were touching. He looked very emotional as he took my hand, smiled and said, "it was the best and wisest decision that I ever made in my life" when I asked him what that was, he said, "it was marrying you". We were heading towards our 60th wedding anniversary and although I have many lovely memories of our life together, that is one of the most precious and treasured memories that I have of him.

He never fully regained his strength after his hospital stay and over the next few weeks his mobility started to deteriorate again. He was no longer able to manage the stairs and so he was confined to his room. The Hospice bed had replaced a double bed and so there was a lot more space in the room and so we turned it into a bedsit for him. All the bedding was white and so I put coloured cushions on his bed during the day so that it looked cosy and didn't look like a hospital ward. I bought him a recliner chair that was much more comfortable for him. I put a chair next to his bed so that I could sit with him and placed some family photographs around the room. With the extra room it meant the family could also sit with him when they visited. We had removed the television as he was no longer able to watch it but he still listened to his music although he no longer sang along with the songs but would just move his index finger in time to the music. He would often ask me to sing to him and so I would sing along with the tracks and it brought a smile to his face.

As his mobility had deteriorated, two of the Hospice physios came out to see if he needed any extra help. They were very impressed with what had been done to the room and said what a pleasant space we had made for him. They asked if they could take a photo of the room to show others as lots of people that they visit, in the same situation, refuse to have a hospital bed as they don't want their home to look like a hospital ward.

They wanted to check his mobility and switched the recliner to lift so that they could get him standing up and onto his walking frame but without help he was only able to take a couple of steps before his knees started to give way. It was decided that he was going to need the use of a hoist for which Andrew and myself would need to have training. However, it turned out that the senior of the two physios knew Andrew and said that he was already well trained in the use of a hoist and that he would be able to train me. They also ordered slider sheets for the bed so he could be turned easily. They were so helpful and kind to Bill which meant a lot to us. The hoist was delivered the next day together with a wheelchair that was specially adapted for use in the bathroom.

When the Community Matron called in to see how things were going, she also passed comments on the room. She asked me how he was and I told her that when he eats, he starts to cough. She said that she would arrange for the Speech Therapist from the Hospice to call in to carry out a swallow test. She came the following morning and asked what sort of meals he was having. He always had porridge for breakfast which I had begun to make smoother so it was easier for him to swallow and any other food I was having to mash up for him. She asked me to get a glass of water and something soft for him to eat like a cake or pudding for him to chew so that she could check his ability to swallow.

She showed me how to mix a jelly like substance into his drinks to make them a little thicker and easier for him to digest as trying to drink water or tea was just making him cough. As she left, she said she would call into the Medical Centre and ask them to send a prescription to the Pharmacy for Nutricia Medical Nutrition which was in the form of a nutritional drink. These were delivered the following day. The Hospice, Medical Centre, Community Matron and District Nurses all liaised with each other and there was no way that I could fault the service we were receiving. I had made the right decision for him to be treated at home under the care of the Hospice rather than the hospital.

A couple of days later I went upstairs to sit with him. As I reached the door I noticed he was leaning to one side and didn't look comfortable, he looked up and said to me "please can you help me", I asked him what was wrong and he said, "I don't want to be like this anymore". What could I say? I knew exactly what he was asking me, he had had enough. There were tears in his eyes and he just looked so sad. It broke my heart to see him like this, I understood how he felt as he had been through so much over the past 5 years. I went over to him picked the pillow up that had fallen on the floor and made him more comfortable in his chair. I kissed his cheek, hugged him and sat holding his hand. I didn't want to leave his side. This disease is so unbelievably cruel.

I didn't tell the family what he had said to me because I knew how much it would have upset them. I spent most days sitting with him and talking about our life together and told him what a good husband and father he had been. I reminded him of the amazing holidays that we had had and talked about some of our favourite places that we had visited, Mexico, Italy and that special trip to Rome to hear Pope John Paul celebrate Mass on Easter Sunday at the Vatican. We had visited, Bethlehem, Jerusalem and the pyramids of Giza from our holidays in Cyprus. I told him how much the surprise trips to Paris for our wedding anniversaries had meant to me and the cruise when we celebrated our silver wedding. He smiled at me and squeezed my hand. I didn't want to leave him sitting alone I just wanted him to remember all the good things about our life together. I think it helped; I hope so anyway. It had been a good life.

The Speech Therapist called in to see him again and I told her it was now difficult for him to swallow his medication; he was on 15 tablets a day. She said that maybe his medication could be taken in liquid form and she arranged for a GP's visit. The Doctor told me to stop all medication as it was no longer of any use to him but she was a little concerned about stopping the Metformin which controlled his diabetes. As it was a Friday, she told me to ring the surgery on Monday morning if his blood sugar levels were above 15 and she would pass his notes over to one of the other Doctors when she got back to the Medical Centre. On Monday his blood sugar level was up to 20 and so I spoke to a Doctor who was expecting my call. I told her he wasn't too well and that we had decided to leave him in bed. She called in and after examining him asked me to come outside of the bedroom so that she could talk to me. She told me he was coming to the end of his life and that he had aspiration pneumonia. Her gut instinct was to call for an ambulance but said she had read on his notes that we didn't want him admitted to hospital. I asked her if he was to go into hospital would they make him better. She said no and felt that he would be more comfortable in his own home. She notified the Hospice so that their nurses and doctors would be available overnight if need be and also that she would arrange for the District Nurses to come in each day. Before she left, she gave me a hug and said how sorry she was. He was no longer able to get out of bed and Andrew and I cared for him together.

I remember his final days so vividly. None of our children were in the country at the time and I was here alone when I was told by the Doctor that he was coming to the end of his life and that his family should be contacted. Alison was at her home in Spain, David and Stephen both in Tenerife. For the first time ever, their holidays had overlapped by two days. Previously they had always made sure that their holidays didn't clash and that I wouldn't be alone and without support. It had been arranged for Alison to stay with me for those two days but her son in Spain had been involved in a road accident and was in hospital. I had told her that I was ok and that her place was with him. I had no idea then that the end was so near and would come so quickly. I sent them all messages telling them they needed to come home. They got the earliest flights possible to be here, in the home where they had been brought up, so that he would be surrounded by the family that he had loved and cared for.

Morphine was kept in the bedroom, in a locked case, should it be needed. Late one evening he was very restless and we thought he might be in pain so Alison informed the Hospice and they sent out two nurses. He was given an injection and they waited for it to take affect before they left. As we were no longer able to give him food or liquid, we had a jelly like substance that we could give him on a spoon. We used sponges dipped into water so that we could swab his lips and the insides of his mouth. When Andrew finished his care in the evenings, he asked if he could just sit with him for a while. He was so kind and gentle with him in those final days and he seemed to have grown genuinely fond of him.

I'll never forget how our grandchildren came in each evening to spend time with him, they were devastated. They would take his hand and kiss him on the forehead and say their name, so he knew which of them was sitting beside him. Whenever Dannii came in to see him she would always say "hello handsome". I never left his side and barely slept that last week. He was surrounded by so much love. Fr Michael, a Franciscan priest, fellow countryman and friend of 18 years, was here to give the last rites. Within 10 minutes of leaving the room so that I could make him tea before he left, Bill took his last breath with just Alison sitting beside him and I felt cheated. Had he waited to be anointed and for when I had left the room before he took that last breath? Did he want to spare me the pain of being beside him and holding his hand as he left us? Doing what he thought was best for me right to the end.

On the days and weeks since he died, I've wondered did I do all that I could for him? Did he know how much I loved him? I tried to do everything that I thought he would have wanted and was so glad that I had made the decision to care for him at home right to the end. It was the right decision and what he would have wanted. Would I do it all again? In a heartbeat.

Grief for me didn't just come at the end, I guess I've been grieving for a while as I watched the man that I had loved for 63 years gradually drift away from me, although in reality he was still here. Some days the Bill I knew and loved would surface for a while and say a few precious words to me, he would take my hand, thank me for helping him, smile and tell me that he loved me but then in the blink of an eye he would return to that other place and his eyes would take on that glazed look and it would seem that he was looking straight through me. Those precious moments that we shared were so special and I felt privileged to have had that time with him and the strength to care for him.

On those nights when I lie in bed and sleep is far away, he is always in my thoughts and as I turn my head and see the empty pillow beside me, I know I have to accept that he is not coming back. If only there could be just one more day for another hug, another kiss and to hear him say 'I love you' one more time but it's not to be and I have to learn to move on to a life without him. I can only hope and pray that there really is a God, there is a heaven and there is a life hereafter where we will spend eternity together.

26

A FINAL GOODBYE

A funeral Mass was held in the church where our marriage was blessed on the occasion of our ruby wedding anniversary. This was followed by a cremation where our granddaughter read the following poem:-

Granddad

Our Granddad kept a garden, a garden of the heart.
He planted all the good things that gave our lives their start.
He turned us to the sunshine and encouraged us to dream,
fostering and nurturing the seeds of self-esteem.

When the winds and rain came, he protected us enough but
not too much because he knew we'd stand
up strong and tough.
His constant good example always taught
us right from wrong,
markers for our pathway that will last a lifetime long.

We are our Granddad's garden; we are his legacy.

THANK YOU, GRANDDAD, WE LOVE YOU

Refreshments were served at a favourite pub on the Downs and as the afternoon turned to evening, the Irish contingent made sure this would be a 'Wake' to be remembered and one that he would have loved to have been in the thick of, surrounded by his family and kin.

In May the following year we took him back to the land of his birth and the Glens of Antrim where we scattered his ashes on the banks of the river just above the 'Ess-na-Crub' waterfall in the Glenariff Forest Park. It was his favourite place in Northern Ireland and one that held many happy memories for him and where he wanted his final resting place to be. Some of his ashes had already been scattered on the grave in Milltown Cemetery in Belfast where his grandparents, mother and brother Gerry are buried.

In June we had a small ceremony in our back garden for his great granddaughters who had been too young to be at his funeral but wanted to say their own goodbyes. They watched as we buried a heart shaped container with the remainder of his ashes in a pot where we had planted a weeping cherry tree in his memory. Each of them placed white pebbles onto the earth and scattered red rose petals. They then released helium balloons and called out "Goodbye, Grandad, we love you" as they continued to wave until the balloons were out of sight.

The garden was his pride and joy and he spent years getting it to the stage it is at today. With the help of a gardener to do the heavier jobs for me, I am determined to carry on where he left off and make sure it is not just a garden that he would be proud of but a memory of the work he put into it over the years and the happy times we spent relaxing in it. It's where I feel closest to him, it is a place where as a family, we celebrated birthdays, summer barbecues and entertained our friends. His bench is of great sentimental value to the family as over the years he would sit and chat there firstly with our children and then with our grandchildren. Whenever they visited, they always knew where to find him, he would be in the garden and they would make a beeline for the bench where they would sit and listen to the tales he would tell them. In the summer evenings I sit on that same bench, that now has a plaque in his memory and remember the special moments spent with him there.

Since his passing, the music from his iPod that had given him so much comfort, 24 hours a day, continued to play. I couldn't bear to turn it off, it was like I was still holding onto a part of him but six months had passed and it was now time for me to let him go and so it was finally switched off. I had done all that I had set out to do. I hope it was enough!

Being a carer was the hardest thing that I have ever had to do in my life. I was exhausted not only physically but mentally too. It was soul destroying. Caring for someone with dementia can stretch you to the limits, you certainly need to be committed, you can't go into it half-heartedly because it just won't work. It's a big commitment to make. There were many times when I thought I couldn't go on but I was fortunate, I was reasonably fit and had family support. I knew I had made the right choice not just for me but for him also.

27

THREE MORE YEARS OF GRIEF

Little did I know then that there would be three more years of grief that I would have to face. My sister-in-law June died just three months after Bill in February 2019 and so my elder brother John, like me, was left alone. At the start of the first lockdown of the Covid pandemic his daughter, bought him a laptop so that we could keep in touch by Skype. He was not in good health, had poor mobility, lived alone and had carers three times a day. It was good for both of us as the country went into lockdown. We would chat very often for up to 2 hours a day and he enjoyed the contact as it was like we were sitting in the same room and so it was company for him and good for me too. He would often laugh and say to me, "are you making the coffee this morning?"

We would discuss what was in the news and put the world to rights. Going down memory lane was another thing that helped us pass the time and we would chat about our childhood and growing up during the war years. Although he was 86, he had an amazing memory and was able to tell me about things that I was too young to remember and about how tough life was for our parents bringing up three children during such hard times; especially with food rationing both during the war and for several years after. I remembered running to the Anderson shelter as a 3-year-old, which was shared with our next-door neighbour, when the siren sounded indicating an air raid. Being three years older than me he recalled watching the dog fights in the sky as our pilots battled with the German aircraft.

In October 2020 the husband of Bill's youngest sister died in Ireland. Three months later in early February 2021, he was followed by his wife, my sister-in-law Helen who was Bill's youngest sister and the baby he had cared for when he was just a young boy. Due to the pandemic, it wasn't possible to go to see her or attend the funeral and as sad as I felt, I couldn't grieve because everything seemed so unreal.

In May 2021 a second brother-in-law in Ireland died from a heart attack. He had been in a care home in Northern Ireland with Alzheimer's for a number of years. I had been able to visit him on my last trip to Ireland and was delighted that he had remembered me, even though we had not seen each other for such a long time. His wife, Rita, Bill's other sister, died just a few weeks later. My two beautiful Irish sisters-in-law had been like the sisters I never had and I was devastated at their loss. It was just too much to take in and not being able to visit or attend any of their funerals was just more grief to bottle up.

The Skype calls with John continued and helped me get through this sad time in my life as they brought us closer together and it was good to have that contact with him. You tend to drift apart from your siblings once you are married and move away from the area you were born in, as you are occupied bringing up your own families. I guess once both parents die the link between you temporarily gets broken but in your later years and when your own children have left home, the link is re-established and you become closer again and so it was with John and me.

However, in July the day came when there was no call from him. I received a message from his daughter to say that he had felt poorly during the night, called an ambulance and had been admitted to hospital. A couple of days later I was told that his kidneys were failing and that his body was beginning to shut down. When the call came to say that he had passed, it hit me hard; I hadn't been able to visit him due to Covid restrictions still being in place in hospitals and so I was unable to say a last goodbye. The daily Skype calls had brought us closer together. If only they had Skype in heaven so that I could talk to him just one more time and tell him that I loved him.

I knew that his funeral was going to be a tough one for me. There had been so much sadness in my life over the past few years. John was a life-long jazz fan and we followed his coffin into the church to Ella Fitzgerald and Louis Armstrong's rendition of 'Summertime'. The church was old and very small and the music seemed to bounce off the walls; I had goosebumps. I had to bite my lip and fight back the tears that I knew were so near to the surface. He had spent 7 years in the Royal Navy and so the hymn chosen was Abide With Me. We followed the coffin out of the church to Louis Armstrong singing 'We Have All The Time In The World' but in fact that time is all too short. It was just too much for me and I could no longer hold it all together. I had tried so hard to be strong for so long but I had reached breaking point and could no longer hold so much grief inside of me even though I knew it would be hard for my children to see me break down.

I walked out of the church alone, completely unaware of anything or anyone around me only that I could feel my whole body shaking and thinking to myself, I need to get away from here. I felt someone touch my arm and heard

Steve's voice saying, 'are you alright mum?' to which I replied, 'no, I'm not'. It was at that stage I had a complete melt down. I cried so hard and thought I would never stop. My younger brother's wife held me tight in her arms and encouraged me to release all the grief that I had held in for the past 3 years. I felt I had lost so much; it had started with the loss of Bill and bottling my feelings up so that I could be strong for the rest of the family, 3 months later June, John's wife had died. The next thing was the Covid pandemic followed shortly after by the first lockdown and that couldn't have come at a worse time for me as we were so limited in what we could do and who we could see. This had been followed by the deaths of Bill's family in Ireland, his two sisters and their husbands all within such a short space of time and then the loss of my eldest brother.

For a week after John's funeral, I never moved from the settee. I had no motivation; so much had been taken away from me in such a short period of time and I just didn't want to carry on feeling like this, with so much sadness in my life. I could feel myself slowly going downhill and knew I had to pull myself together. I felt like I was drowning in my sorrow. It was sink or swim time for me and I had to start swimming to survive. I knew I had to get back out there and get on with my life or what I had left of it and I knew it wouldn't be easy. I know that is what Bill would want me to do and if he is looking down on me and I'm sure that he is, he would be saying: -

Go out there and live life to the full for both of us. I will be right beside you and always remember,

I'LL LOVE YOU FOREVER

28

EPILOGUE

Grief is a love that has nowhere to go. Grief and love are like two sides of one coin without love there is no grief. Grieving doesn't stop because the love for that special person never stops and the memory of them will stay with you forever. When Bill left, he took a big part of my heart with him but how lucky was I that we had 63 wonderful years together. I spend a lot of time on my own and as I play the music we enjoyed together and remember the good times; I feel his presence and so I am never lonely because I feel he is watching over me. It's when I am in a room full of people that I feel the loneliness because he isn't there by my side like he was so many times throughout our life together and it is at times like this when I really feel his loss.

Spending a lifetime with the one you love and then losing them is heart breaking. I had lost so many loved ones in such a short space of time that I didn't feel I could go on. No one can live for ever and you realise that life is all too short. I know he wouldn't want me to be sad and lonely, he would want me to move on to a life without him.

I saw an advert for Stroll Classes that came up on my Facebook feed and the classes were being held less than a 10-minute walk from my home and as a non-driver they would be easy for me to get to and I wouldn't have to rely on anyone else. Maybe this was the first step I needed to take. I rang the number given for more information and spoke to Tracey Allen of 'TJ's Jive'. I explained my situation and how I had lost my husband and several family members over a short space of time. I was at a very low point in my life and as hard as it was, I knew I had to move on but I thought that I might be too old to start a dance class at 83 but she was very encouraging and told me that her mother was 87 and in the advanced class. This gave me the push I needed. However, I nearly backed out on the morning of the first class. It was the first time in a long time of going out socially on my own and into a room full of strangers. I wasn't sure I was ready to take that step and was on the verge of turning around and going home but she saw me and said to come in.

The others in the group were very friendly and took the time to come over and introduce themselves. I enjoyed the class, had got over the first hurdle and over the next two weeks I began to feel more at ease. Stroll is very similar to Line Dancing and a lot of the music we danced to was from the 50s/60s/70s, my era. Bill and I had always loved dancing and we used to jive, rock and roll style in our early days together and almost up into our 70s when we attended parties and family weddings. When it was announced a few weeks later that a Beginners Jive Course was to start, I was really interested but thought I might be really pushing it at my age to start jiving again but Tracey and her assistant Michelle Robinson assured me that there are more people of 60 and above jiving than there are younger people and suggested I give it a try. I had nothing to lose. It was slightly different to the jiving I was used to in our rock and roll days but I soon got back into the rhythm of it, I progressed each week and loved every minute of it. It brought back many happy memories for me and I just loved the music, the music of our courting days. Monday evenings were taken up with the 'Jive' class whilst I continued with 'Stroll' classes on Tuesday mornings. I made new friends and got a lot of my confidence back. Joining 'TJ's' was the best thing that could have happened to me and the very thing I needed to get back on track. I can't thank Tracey and Michelle enough for their encouragement and support. I feel like I have been given a new lease on life and I would recommend it to anyone, young or old and especially those who are lonely and find themselves in the same position that I was in.

I know Bill would be happy for me and that he will be looking down on me with that smile on his face that I remember so well and miss so much. I still think of him every minute of every day and that will never, ever change.

After 52 years I am still living in our 'forever home' and it is where I will spend my final years. It is the home where we raised our children and where they brought their children to visit us. A home that we had shared together for so many years and where we had fulfilled our ambitions and our dreams. It has always been a house full of love and happiness and one full of so many wonderful memories. It is a home where I feel surrounded by his love and still feel his presence. We were lucky; we had a marriage that was made in heaven; we were truly Blessed.

I return to Ireland
It's the 28th May 2022, my 84th birthday and I am in Ireland for a family wedding. I am booked into a hotel on the Killeavy Castle Estate in Newry where the reception is being held. I have a large twin room for single use and it is beautifully decorated and luxurious. It is on the ground floor overlooking the lovely gardens where peacocks wander and

the view is stunning. Outside the sliding doors there is a small patio with a table and two chairs. I open the door and step outside and suddenly feel very emotional and have teared up. I feel his presence and the comfort of his arm around my shoulder but as I turn to look up at him, I realise he is not with me physically but I know in my heart his spirit is. We had been to all the family weddings together over the space of many years but this was the first Irish wedding I had attended without him and what a wedding it was turning out to be. The usual three days of Irish hospitality and a celebration that he would have loved to have been part of.

November 2022

This past week has been a difficult one for me as I received the news that Bill's youngest brother Jim had also passed from Lewy Body Dementia. He was the first one of the family that I had met back in 1957 when he came to London looking for work as Bill had done before him. It is sad that the family I had married into have now all departed this world in such a short space of time but I take some comfort in knowing that they are now reunited.

June 2024

I am back in Ireland. This time for the wedding of our Godson Chris and his partner Niamh who have returned to Ireland to get married. They had moved to Australia several years ago to start out on a new life together. Over the years Chris had often said to us that if we made it to his wedding day then we would have been there for all the most important occasions in his life. His baptism as his Godparents, his first Holy Communion and his Confirmation with Bill as his sponsor. Unfortunately, Bill never made it to his wedding but I am fortunate enough to be here on this special day and felt honoured when I was asked to sign as a witness to his signature on the wedding certificate. On entering the church, the first thing I noticed, on a small table beside the altar, was a framed photograph of Bill. It was a very emotional moment for me. Beside it were photographs of Chris's grandparents, Bill's sister Rita and her husband John and also Niamh's grandfather. Loved ones that although had passed were very much remembered on this their special day.

29

THE TREE OF LIFE

Our family has deep roots and many branches.

Throughout its life the branches of a tree wither
and die but with the wonders of nature new
growth appears to replace those branches
that are no longer there.

Just like our own family tree, as the older
generation reaches maturity, they begin to
weaken and lose their strength and so the time comes for
them to leave us to make room for new life to appear.

As you look on our Tree of Life know that the
memories of those we have lost will never die,
will stay with us always and will remain
in our hearts forever.

In time new life will start to appear at the
bottom of our tree as another generation will
be born and so life on our tree continues.

Rita Beggins

Since Bill's passing Zoey, a new Great Granddaughter
has arrived to join our tree and so the family
we started continues to grow

30

RESEARCH

During my research, I read an article by the BMC Health Service that was published in October 2019, a year after Bill's passing and found that although people with dementia covered a significant number of health and social care users, until recently in the United Kingdom, there were no prescribed standards for dementia education and training.

It was reported in the Nursing Times in May 2014 that all NHS staff were to receive specialist dementia training by 2018 but according to the above it appears that this didn't happen at that time. That is scandalous.

When I was chatting to a friend who is a nurse, about the poor care that Bill had received on a dementia ward, she told me that at that time they were only just starting to give nurses the required training. I wonder how far the NHS has come with that? Do they just look on dementia patients as being old and nearing the end of their lives anyway and so think that they are not worth wasting resources on? It needs to be treated as a priority after all any one of us, rich or poor, can be stricken down with this disease.

One of the big things the National Health Service has failed upon, in my opinion, is the care of the elderly and I still hear of this being the case in the many Care Homes around the country where the quality of some staff is not up to the required standards.

The impact of dementia on individuals and families is devastating and with an aging population it will only get worse as more and more are struck down with the disease. If only a cure could be found. Although a lot of research is being done by the Alzheimer's Society, Dementia UK and other bodies, Governments around the world need to plough more money into research because as people are living longer more and more are going to suffer with this dreadful disease.

Our Government always seem to be able to find the money to waste on some unnecessary project or hairbrained scheme while the NHS not only needs more money invested into it, but it also needs a complete revamp as it is not being run efficiently. They hand out millions in foreign aid every year and yet cannot find the millions needed for our own elderly who have worked all their lives and paid into a system that is no longer fit for purpose. Unfortunately, they have become a forgotten generation and sadly nobody seems to care.